# The Super Easy Keto Slow Cooker Cookbook

250 Quick & Easy 5-Ingredients Recipes for Busy and Novice that Cook Themselves

2-Weeks Keto Meal Plan – Lose Up to 16 Pounds

By

Fiona Griffith

# TABLE OF CONTETS

# INTRODUCTION

Do you know that slow cooking is one of the most straightforward cooking techniques that can yield some of the most mouthwatering results? A slow cooker allows you to put each of the ingredients directly into one pot for a mouthwatering recipe, give it a good stir and then leave it to cook slowly for hours. You will enjoy the mouthwatering scents that waft through your home all day long. You can eat the meal with zero other preparations needed at mealtime. It's just not getting any better. Tender meat from the bone, cold stews, slow cooking is the ultimate in natural food.

Slow cooking is undoubtedly a favorite and preferred cooking technique for many reasons. Nevertheless, you will need to be mindful that these devices can be bulky and may need some space inside the cabinet. However, there are positive aspects to the size. For prominent families and groups of people, they are excellent for cooking. Usually, the sheer volume of most slow cookers means you can have a lot more food than you might need for a typical family meal (its main meal can feed 6-8 people regularly). The beautiful thing about it means that for another day, you will be able to freeze any remains.

Slow cookers can also save some costs because low-priced meat cuts are best given that the slow cooking process tenderizes the meat all day long. Moreover, these types of lower-priced meat cuts typically have more moisture compared to leaner beef cuts, making them ideal for slow cooking.

For a slow cooker, you don't need to spend too much cash as there are plenty of great ones for sale out there at a reasonable cost. I advise you to buy a slow cooker with a volume of between 5-7 liters plus a low, high, and automatic setting. No more fancy features than these few simple settings are required.

Many delicious slow cooker recipes are available online so that you won't get lost for choices for the meal. While beef and lamb work particularly well, chicken, pork and seafood, soups, roasts, and a host of other tasty items can also be used to cook them.

Slow cooking, in short, is a safe way to cook delicious family meals. Get a slow cooker and start experimenting with today's wide range of recipes to choose from.

# BENEFITS OF SLOW COOKING

A typical kitchen appliance is a slow cooker. Slow cooking is a primary cooking method that helps to preserve nutrients and flavor. Even when baking, delicate foods like fruit, fish, and veg will not break up as much. A slow cooker can make a delicious treat for the cheapest cut of meat.

As the slow cooker cooks at a very low wattage, energy efficiency is improved, and the long cooking cycle can tenderize even the cheapest meat.

A slow cooker consists of a heating element and a large ceramic pot, often referred to as a crockpot (usually with adjustable heat settings). These are available in sizes that are appropriate for individuals, couples, or families. They are ideal for cooking spicy curries, heart-filled casseroles, stews, or soups, but you can't do it all. To cook delicious, creamy porridge overnight, some families use a slow cooker.

Having dinner ready day after day may turn into a dull and tedious job that you may well get tired after a long period. At times when you are tired of cooking for the family, you may want to consider something about slow cooking in these cases. Slow cooking has many advantages, including saving time, locking in the flavor, and making your mealtime flexible.

Slow cooking has many benefits for you and your family, and one of the main advantages we can all take is being able to save time by simmering your meal instead of preparing it another way. It allows you to devote all your attention to this process. All you need to do when you slow cook your meal is to make the dish in the slow cooker and then let it cook on its own. You don't always have to watch it, and when the time needed to prepare your dish has expired, you can come back to it. It's going to be ready to eat at that time, and you are not going to have to think about cooking anything else to go with it. Your family will appreciate the fast meal, and you will understand the trouble that has been saved by not having to take care of the meal while cooking.

Another benefit of slow cooking is that less liquid is lost due to the sealed environment when you slow cook something. Your food is going to be more moist and sweet than cooking it in a conventional oven or microwave. The slow process of cooking enables the moisture to be locked in so that it does not evaporate. It collects only inside the compartment where the food being cooked absorbs it. Which means the meats are going to be juicier and more tender.

Finally, you don't have to serve it immediately after it's finished when you slowly cook your meal. You can leave it to sit down, and when they have the time or when they are hungry enough to eat, your family can help themselves. This is a huge time saver for you as you don't need to set the table or prepare side items for the meal right now. You can sit back and relax and enjoy the meal at your own pace for your family. What's better than that?

# BREAKFAST RECIPES

## 1. SAVORY BREAKFAST SAUSAGE

### Ingredients

- 1/8 tsp cayenne pepper
- 1 tsp sage
- 220g ground chicken
- 220g ground pork
- 1/4 tsp celery seed, nutmeg, garlic powder, onion powder, paprika
- 1/2 tsp salt, black thyme pepper

### Instructions

1. Knead with your hands after mixing all the ingredients in a bowl.
2. Make six patty hamburgers, wrap and freeze them in saran wrap. We're going to use these for the next six days, so if you think the meat is going to stay fresh, you are not going to have to freeze them, but I just did it in case.

**Prep Time** – 10min

**Servings** – 4

**Macros** - 185 calories 12.81g fat 0.25g carbs 0.2g fiber 0.04g sugar 16.17g protein

## 2. AVOCADO BUN BREAKFAST BURGER

### Ingredients

- One avocado
- One egg
- 1 tbsp sesame seeds, mayo pinch salt, pepper,
- One slice tomato
- 1 tbsp olive oil
- One lettuce leaf

### Instructions

1. Place the avocado horizontally on its side and slice it right in the middle to make sure that you don't cut it at an awkward angle. When sliced, pick the seed carefully and spoon out of the flesh carefully.
2. Attach the sausage breakfast and cook 1-2 minutes on each side until well cooked on medium-low heat after heating the oil in a non-stick skillet. In the skillet, crack the egg open, turn the heat down, cover, and cook on the sunny side. Make sure that the white egg is fully cooked. Place the lower half of the avocado on a plate, spoon some mayo in the avocado hole, top with lettuce, tomato, sausage, add the egg carefully and top with the top of the avocado. Sprinkle some salt, pepper, and sesame seeds.

**Preparation Time** 15 min

**Servings** - 2

**Macros** - 717 calories 61.36g fat 20.11g carbs 14.6g fiber 2.88g sugar 27.41g protein

## 3. AVOCADO CREAM & ZOODLES

### Ingredients

- One zucchini
- 1/2 avocado (100g)
- 20 basil leaves
- 1.5 tbsp olive oil
- Three brown mushrooms (30g)
- One garlic clove
- 1 tsp lemon juice
- 1/4 tsp salt

**Instructions**

1. Spiralize your zucchini. Slice the mushrooms in half.
2. Place the avocado, basil, 1 tbsp of olive oil, garlic, lemon juice, and salt in a stick blender cup. Press the button on the blender until all is super smooth and delicious for about a minute.
3. In a frying pan, add 1/2 tbsp of olive oil and cook until tender. Attach the zucchini noodles and cook until they get warm for just a minute or so. 4. Add the cream of the avocado, blend it all, and serve.

**Prep Time** – 10 Min

**Servings** - 5

**Macros** - 383 calories 35.34g fat 18g carbs 9.4g fiber 4.74g sugar 5.46g protein.

## 4. CLASSIC BACON AND EGGS

**Ingredients**

- Eight large eggs
- 5 ounces sliced bacon
- 12-16 cherry tomatoes
- 1/4 cup chopped fresh parsley

**Instruction**

1. To make it crispy, fry the bacon in a pan on light heat. Put aside on a plate. Leave the rendered fat in the pan.
2. Utilize the same pan to fry the eggs. Place it over light heat and crack your eggs into the bacon grease. You can also break them into a measuring cup and carefully pour into the pan to avoid splattering of hot oil.
3. Cook the eggs to your taste. For sunny side up — you can fry the egg on one side and close the pan with a cover to ensure they are well cooked.
4. You can easily add salt and pepper to add more taste.

**Servings** - 4

**Preparation Time** - 10 - 15 min

**Macros** - 322.35 Calories, 22.15g Fats, 3.1g Net Carbs, and 24.23g Protein.

## 5. BOILED EGGS WITH MAYONNAISE

**Ingredients**

- Eight eggs
- 8 tbsp mayonnaise
- Two avocados (optional)

**Instructions**

1. Boil water in a bowl
2. Optional: use an egg piercer to make tiny holes in the shells. Those help eggs crack as they cook.
3. Put the eggs carefully in the bowl.
4. For soft-boiled eggs, boil the eggs for 5–6 minutes, for medium 6–8 minutes and for hard-boiled eggs for 8–10 minutes.

5. Use mayonnaise to serve.

**Preparation Time** - 10 min

**Servings** - 4

**Macros** (per serving) - Calories 316 kcal, Protein 11g, Fat 29g, Net Carbs 1g

## 6. KETO-MEXICAN SCRAMBLES EGGS

### Ingredients

- 1 oz. butter
- One scallion, finely chopped
- Two pickled jalapeños, finely chopped
- One tomato, finely chopped, six eggs
- 3 oz. shredded cheese, salt, and pepper

### Instructions

1. Using a frying pan, melt the butter with light heat.
2. Add scallions, jalapeños, and tomatoes, and fry for 3-4 minutes.
3. Mix the eggs and pour them into the pan. Scramble for 2 minutes adds cheese and seasonings.

**Servings** – 4

**Preparation Time** 10 – 15 min

**Macros** – Calories 229 kcal, Protein 14g, Fat 19g, Net carbs 2g

## 7. KETO AVOCADO EGGS WITH BACON SAILS

### Ingredients

- Two medium egg Egg (hard-boiled)
- 1/2 avocado(s) Avocado
- 1 tbsp Olive oil
- Two medium slice Bacon
- One pinch Salt and pepper (to taste)

### Instructions

1. Cook the eggs and let it cool
2. Separate the eggs (as you would for deviled eggs). Take out the yolk and combine with the avocado, oil and salt and pepper to taste.
3. Keep the bacon in the oven or use a frying pan for 5 -7 minutes at 180 degrees to make it crispy.
4. With a spoon, carefully add the mixture back into the egg and set the bacon sail! Enjoy!

**Servings** - 4

**Preparation Time** - 15 - 20 min

**Macros** - Calories 157 kcal, Fat 14g, Protein 6g, Net carbs 1g.

## 8. SCRAMBLED EGGS WITH BASIL AND BUTTER

### Ingredients

- 2 tbsp coconut cream or coconut milk
- salt
- 1 oz. butter
- 2 oz. shredded cheese (optional)
- 2 tbsp fresh basil
- Two eggs

### Instructions

1. First, you need to melt the butter with low heat.
2. Mix the eggs, cream, and salt in a small bowl. Whist the mixture gently and pour inside the pan.
3. Stir with a spatula from the edge towards the center until the eggs are

scrambled. I like it soft and creamy, not with a crisp surface, which means often stirring on lower heat. You can choose to remove the pan from the heat when you add the mixture; this is usually enough heat to cook creamy soft-shambled eggs.

**Servings** - 1

**Preparation Time** - 5 - 7 min

**Macros** (per serving) - Fat 42g, Protein13g, Net carbs 2g, Calories 427 kcal.

## 9. KETO EGG MUFFINS

### Ingredients

- Two scallions, finely chopped
- salt and pepper
- 6 oz. shredded cheese
- 12 eggs
- Six cooked strips sugar-free bacon, crumbled

### Instructions

1. Prepare the oven for 175 degrees.
2. Arrange a muffin tin with an insertable baking cups.
3. Add scallions and chorizo to the base of the tin.
4. Mix the eggs with pesto, salt, and pepper. Add the cheese and stir.
5. Make the scallions and chorizo have the batter on top.
6. Based on the size of the muffin tin, bake for 15 to 20 mins.

**Servings** - 6

**Preparation Time** - 25 min

**Macros** (per servings) - Fat 26g, Protein 23g, Calories 336 kcal, Net carbs 2g.

## 10. KETO CHEESE OMELET

### Ingredients

- 3 oz. butter
- Six eggs
- salt and pepper to taste
- 7 oz. shredded cheddar cheese

### Instructions

1. Mix the eggs smoothly then blend in half of the cheddar.
2. Next, melt the butter in a hot frying pan and pour the egg mixture from 1 and leave for a few minutes.
3. Reduce the heat and cook the egg mixture continuously till it is cooked. Add the remaining shredded cheese.
4. Fold the content and serve immediately.

**Preparation Time** - 15 min

**Servings** - 2

**Macros** (per serving) - Fat 80g, protein 40g, Net carbs 4g, Calories 897 kcal.

## 11. KETO COCONUT PORRIDGE

### Ingredients

- One egg, beaten
- 1 tbsp coconut flour
- One pinch psyllium husk powder
- One pinch salt
- 1 oz. butter or coconut oil
- 4 tbsp coconut cream

### Instructions

1. Mix the egg, coconut flour, psyllium husk powder in a small powder.

2. Melt the butter and coconut cream over low heat. Slowly whisk the egg mixture to achieve a thick creamy texture.
3. Add some fresh berries to your porridge and enjoy it. Serve with coconut milk or cream.

**Preparation Time** - 10 min

**Servings** - 1

**Macros** (per serving) - Fat 49g, Protein 9g, Net carbs 4g, Calories 486 kcal.

## 12. NO BREAD KETO BREAKFAST SANDWICH

### Ingredients

- 2 tbsp butter
- Four eggs
- salt and pepper
- 1 oz. smoked deli ham
- 2 oz. cheddar cheese or provolone cheese, cut in thick slices

### Instructions

1. Put butter in a medium heat frying pan, fry the egg on both sides and add salt and pepper.
2. Use a fried egg as the base for each "sandwich." Place the ham/pastrami/cold cuts on each stack next, and then add the cheese. Top off each stack with a fried egg. Leave cheese t melt on low heat if you want.
3. Serve immediately after sprinkling a few drops of tabasco sauce.

**Preparation Time** - 15 min

**Servings** - 2

**Macros** (per serving) - Fat 30g, Protein 20g, Net carbs 2g, Calories 354 kcal.

## 13. SALAD SANDWICHES

### Ingredients

- 2 oz. Romaine lettuce or baby gem lettuce
- ½ oz. butter
- 1 oz. Edam cheese
- ½ avocado
- One cherry tomatoes

### Instructions

1. Use the lettuce as a base of the toppings after rinsing thoroughly.
2. Smear butter on the lettuce leaves and slice the cheese, avocado, and tomato and add on top.

**Preparation Time** - 5 min

**Servings** - 1

**Macros** (per serving) - Fat 34g, Protein 10g, Net carbs 3g, Calories 374 kcal.

## 14. KETO SCRAMBLED EGGS WITH HALLOUMI CHEESE

Ingredients

- 2 tbsp olive oil
- 3 oz. halloumi cheese, diced
- Two scallions, chopped, 4 oz. bacon, diced
- 4 tbsp fresh parsley, chopped
- Four eggs, salt, and pepper
- ½ cup pitted olives

### Instructions

1. Heat olive oil on medium-high in a frying pan and fry halloumi,

scallions, and bacon until you get a browned texture.

2. Whisk together parsley, eggs, salt, and pepper in a small bowl.
3. Lower the heat, pour the egg mixture into the frying pan over the bacon and cheese. Add the olives and stir afterward for a couple of minutes.

**Servings** - 2

**Preparation Time** - 25 min

**Macros** - Net carbs: 4 g), Fiber: 1 g, Fat: (59 g) , Protein: (28 g), Calories : 663 kcal

## 15. KETO-MEXICAN SCRAMBLED EGGS

### Ingredients

- 1 oz. butter
- One scallion, finely chopped
- Two pickled jalapeños, finely chopped
- One tomato, finely chopped
- Six eggs
- 3 oz. shredded cheese
- salt and pepper

### Instructions

1. Melt the butter with medium heat in a large frying pan.
2. Add scallions, jalapeños, and tomatoes, and fry for 3-4 minutes.
3. Pour the egg into the pan after mixing it correctly. Scramble for 2 minutes adds cheese and seasonings.

**Preparation Time** - 15 min

**Servings** - 4

**Macros** (per serving) - Net carbs: 2 g, Fat: 18 g Protein: 14 g kcal: 229

## 16. KETO BREAKFAST TAPAS

### Ingredients

- 8 oz. prosciutto
- 8 oz. chorizo
- 4 oz. cucumber
- 4 oz. cheddar cheese
- 2 oz. red bell peppers

### Instructions

1. Split the cold cuts, cheese, and vegetables into sticks or cubes.
2. Get a plate and arrange, serve, and enjoy.

**Preparation time** - 5 min

**Servings** - 4

**Macros** (per serving) - Net carbs: 5 g, Fiber: 1 g, Fat: 57 g, Protein: 30 g, kcal: 664

## 17. MOZZARELLA BASE CAFFEE

### Ingredients

- 1 Egg
- 1/2 Cup Mozzarella Cheese

### Instructions

1. Heat Waffle Maker
2. Whisk Egg
3. Add Cheese and other ingredients
4. Cook 4 minutes
5. Remove and Cool 2-3 minutes

**Preparation Time** - 6 min

**Servings** - 2

**Macros** (per serving) - Calories – 76 kcal, Net Carbs – 0.7g, Total Fat – 2.4g, Protein – 12.1g

## 18. SAVORY CHEDDAR CHAFFEE

### Ingredients

- 1 Egg
- 1/2 cup Cheddar Cheese

### Instructions

1. Heat Waffle Maker
2. Whisk Egg
3. Add Cheese and other ingredients
4. Cook 4 minutes
5. Remove and Cool 2-3 minutes

**Preparation Time** - 6 min

**Servings** - 2

**Macros** (per serving) - Calories – 150 kcal, Net Carbs – 1.1g, Total Fat – 11.8g, Protein – 9.6g

## 19. BLUEBERRY CHAFFEE

### Ingredients

- 1 Egg
- 1/2 Cup Mozzarella Cheese
- 1 Tablespoon Smashed Blueberries

### Instructions

1. Heat Waffle Maker
2. Whisk Egg
3. Add Cheese and other ingredients
4. Cook 4 minutes
5. Remove and Cool 2-3 minutes

**Preparation Time** - 6 min

**Servings** - 2

**Macros** (per serving) - Calories – 79 kcal, Net Carbs – 1.4g, Total Fat – 2.4g, Protein – 12.1g

## 20. PARMESAN GARLIC CHAFFEE

### Ingredients

- 1 Egg
- 1/2 Cup Shredded Cheddar or Mozzarella
- 1/4 cup Parmesan Cheese
- 1/4 Teaspoon Minced Garlic
- 1/8 Teaspoon Italian Seasoning

### Instructions

1. Heat Waffle Maker
2. Whisk Egg
3. Add Cheese and other ingredients
4. Cook 4 minutes
5. Remove and Cool 2-3 minutes

**Preparation Time** - 6 min

**Servings** - 2

**Macros** (per serving) - Calories – 192 kcal, Net Carbs – 1.5g, Total Fat – 14.5g, Protein – 13.4g

## 21. STRAWBERRY CHAFFEE

### Ingredients

- 1 Egg
- 1/2 Cup Mozzarella Cheese
- 1 Tablespoon Cream Cheese
- 2 Tablespoons Almond Flour
- 3 Sliced Strawberries

### Instructions

- Heat Waffle Maker
- Whisk Egg
- Add Cheese and other ingredients
- Cook 4 minutes
- Remove and Cool 2-3 minutes

**Preparation Time** - 6 min

**Servings** - 2

**Macros** (per serving) - Calories – 184 kcal, Net Carbs – 3.1g, Total Fat – 6.2g, Protein – 22.6g

## 22. CINNAMON CHAFFLE

### Ingredients

- 1 Egg
- ½ Cup Mozzarella
- ½ Teaspoon Cinnamon
- ½ Teaspoon Vanilla

### Instructions

1. Heat Waffle Maker
2. Whisk Egg
3. Add Cheese and other ingredients
4. Cook 4 minutes
5. Remove and Cool 2-3 minutes

**Preparation Time** - 6 min

**Servings** - 2

**Macros** (per serving) - Calories – 80 kcal, Net Carbs – 1.1g, Total Fat – 2.4g, Protein – 12.1

## 23. BISCUIT AND SAUSAGE GRAVY

### Ingredients

Biscuit:

- 1 cup Almond Flour
- 1/4 cup Coconut Flour
- 1/4 cup butter
- 2 tbsp. Sour Cream
- 1 tsp. Baking Powder
- 1/4 tsp. Salt

Sausage Gravy:

- 1 1/2 cup Heavy Cream
- 1/2 tsp. Guar Gum
- 1/2 lb. Breakfast Sausage
- Salt and Pepper to Taste

### Instructions

1. Combine all ingredients for the biscuits, then set aside.
2. Brown sausage in a pan over medium-high heat. Once finished, add to the slow cooker.
3. Add some heavy cream and salt and pepper to the sausage. Then, add guar gum and whisk together.
4. Roll out biscuits and place them on top of the sausage gravy.
5. Cook on high for 2 hours

**Preparation Time** - 20min

This makes four servings. Each serving:

590.3 Calories - 54.3 Fats (g)

5.8 Net Carbs (g) - 16.0 Protein (g)

## 24. ZUCCHINI BAKED GREEN APPLES

### Ingredients

- 12 oz. Zucchini
- 3/4 cup Water
- One packet Sugar-Free Lime (or Lemon) Jello
- 1 tbsp. Cinnamon, 1 tsp. Nutmeg
- 2 tbsp. Xylitol
- 1/2 cup Heavy Cream

### Instructions

1. Peel zucchini and slice into 1/6" pieces. Using a mandolin will help with speed.

2. Add all the ingredients (except heavy cream) to a slow cooker, and then stir together.
3. Cook on low for about 2 1/2 hours.
4. Add 1/2 cup of some heavy cream and gently mix into the sauce.

**Preparation Time** – 10 min

This makes four servings. Each serving:

148.0 Calories - 12.5 Fats (g) 4.0 Net Carbs (g) - 2.0 Protein (g)

## 25. ARMADILLO EGGS

### Ingredients

- 1 lb. Ground Pork
- 1/4 cup Almond Flour
- 2 tbsp. Parmesan Cheese, Chili Powder, 1 tsp. Garlic Powder, 1/2 tsp. Onion Powder
- 1/4 tsp. Red Pepper Flakes
- Seven small Jalapenos, 3 oz. Cream Cheese, Salt, and Pepper to Taste

### Instructions

1. Mix ground pork with all spices set aside.
2. Chop jalapeno peppers in half, and then de-seed them by scraping innards out with a spoon.
3. Fill half jalapeno pepper with cream cheese, and then replace the other half on top. Repeat.
4. Wrap each jalapeno with the pork mixture.
5. Set all armadillo eggs in the slow cooker and cook for 5 hours on low.

This makes three servings. Each serving:

590.3 Calories - 49.0 Fats (g) 3.8 Net Carbs (g) - 32.0 Protein (g)

**Preparation Time** – 10 min

## 26. ASIAN COUNTRY RIBS

### Ingredients

- 1 tbsp. Sesame Oil and Olive Oil
- 4 tbsp. Soy Sauce
- 3.5 lbs. Country Ribs
- 2 1/2 tbsp. Sambal Olek, 3 tbsp. Reduced Sugar Ketchup
- 1 1/2 tbsp. Rice Wine Vinegar, 2 tsp. Garlic, minced, 1 tsp. Onion Powder and Ginger Powder

### Instructions

1. Combine all ingredients (except country ribs) by mixing with a whisk to create the marinade.
2. In a plastic bag, add marinade and ribs — massage marinade into the bones.
3. Let it sit for 30 minutes, but preferably overnight.
4. Place all ingredients in a slow cooker. Turn on low for 6 hours (or high for 4 hours).
5. Once ribs are tender, remove the lid of the slow cooker and cook on low for another 30 minutes

**Preparation Time** – 10 min

This makes 12 servings. Each serving:

381.2 Calories - 25.7 Fats (g)

0.6 Net Carbs (g) - 33.3 Protein (g)

## 27. CHEESEBURGER MEATBALLS

### Ingredients

- 1 lb. Ground Beef (80/20)

- 12-18 Cheese Cubes (depending on the size of meatballs)
- 1/4 cup Almond Flour
- One large Egg
- 3/4 tsp. Garlic, 1/2 tsp. Onion Powder, 1/4 tsp. Cumin, 1 tsp. Worcestershire Sauce

## Instructions

1. Combine all the ingredients (except for cheese) into a bowl. Mix well.
2. Form meatballs with cheese cubes in the center, making sure there are no holes left in the meatball mixture.
3. Place all meatballs into the slow cooker and cook for 5 hours on low or 3 hours on high.
4. Note: Putting them on high for 30 minutes, then turning to low helps seal the meatballs and helps keep the cheese inside.

This makes five servings. Each serving:

500.0 Calories - 40.0 Fats (g) 1.2 Net Carbs (g) - 32.0 Protein (g)

**Preparation Time** – 15 mins

## 28. CHEESEBURGER PIE

### Ingredients

- 1 lb. Ground Beef, browned with fat drained
- 1/4 cup Mayonnaise
- 4 oz. Cream Cheese, 8 oz. Cheddar Cheese
- Two Large Eggs
- One cube Beef Bouillon Cube, crumbled
- 1/4 tsp. Onion Powder, 1/4 tsp. Garlic Powder, 1 tsp. Dried Minced Onion

## Instructions

1. Grate cheddar cheese, separating half of it for later.
2. In a pan, add all the ingredients (except half the cheese).
3. Press all ingredients into a greased slow cooker.
4. Top with cheese and turn on low for 4-5 hours or high for 3 hours.
5. Garnish with ketchup, mayonnaise, and pickles

**Preparation Time** – 15 mins

This makes six servings. Each serving:

401.5 Calories - 32.5 Fats (g) 1.7 Net Carbs (g) - 24.3 Protein (g)

## 29. CHEESY SAUSAGE AND MUSHROOM SOUP

### Ingredients

- 12 oz. Andouille Sausage, sliced thin, 9 oz. Baby Bella Mushrooms, sliced thin
- 1 tbsp. Olive Oil, 1 tsp. Garlic, minced
- 1 cup Heavy cream, 3 cups Chicken Stock,
- 1 tsp. Guar Gum, 1/8 tsp. Nutmeg
- 8 oz. Cheddar Cheese, shredded, 1/2 medium onion, 1/4 cup butter

### Instructions

1. In a pan over medium-high heat, brown sausage until cooked. Set aside.
2. In the same pan, cook onion and mushroom in the pan until soft.
3. Add stock, nutmeg, garlic, and guar gum into the slow cooker and whisk together until guar gum is incorporated.

4. Add the sausage, onion, mushrooms, and butter into the slow cooker and mix.
5. Cook on low temp for 4 hours or high for 3 hours. Once finished, add the finishing ingredients and stir them together.
6. Cook for an additional 30 minutes without the lid in the slow cooker.

This makes six servings. Each serving:

558.2 Calories - 50.2 Fats (g) 3.5 Net Carbs (g) - 23.5 Protein (g)

**Preparation Time** – 20 mins

## 30. SLOW COOKER BREAKFAST STUFFED PEPPERS

### Ingredients

- 1/2 pound ground breakfast sausage
- Four bell peppers, Six large eggs
- 4 oz Crystal Farms Marble Jack Cheese
- 4 oz fire-roasted chopped green chiles
- 1/8 teaspoon pepper, 1/4 teaspoon salt,

### Instructions

1. Over medium-high heat, brown sausage in a skillet until fully cooked, drain any excess grease.
2. Pour 1/2 cup of water into the bottom of a slow cooker
3. Wash peppers, cut off tops and clean out ribs and seeds and place with the open side up in the slow cooker
4. In a pan, crack eggs and whisk until smooth.

5. Shred cheese using a box grater or food processor
6. Stir sausage, shredded cheese, and green chilies into eggs and add salt and pepper
7. Spoon egg and cheese mixture into each pepper, filling to top (amount of filing you use will vary slightly depending on the size of peppers)
8. Cover and cook for 2-3 hours or 4-6 hours or until the egg is fully set.
9. Top with chopped green onion or cilantro if desired for garnish before serving

**Preparation time** - 10 min

**Servings** - 4

**Macros** - Calories 109, Fat 6g, Saturated Fat 2g, Carbohydrates 4g, Protein 8g

## 31. SLOW COOKER FRENCH TOAST CASSEROLE

### Ingredients

- 8 ounces bread whole grain (about eight slices)
- 1 cup milk 2%, complete or non-dairy
- Six large eggs
- One teaspoon vanilla extract, 1/4 teaspoon salt,1 1/2 teaspoon cinnamon, 1/4 cup brown sugar

### Instructions

1. In a pan, break the rice.
2. Whisk milk, bacon, vanilla, brown sugar, cinnamon, salt together. A verse in the bowl. Make sure the mixture covers the bread fully. Refrigerate for a minimum of 4 hours.

3. Grease the inside of a slow cooker when ready to cook. Remove the mixture and cover it in an even layer. Cook for 8 to 10 hours on the water.

4. If needed, using maple syrup or powdered sugar.

**Preparation Time** - 10 min

**Servings** - 5

**Macros** - Calories 189, Fat 6g, Saturated Fat 2g, Carbohydrates 3g, Protein 6g

## 32. EASY WHITE CHICKEN CHILI

### Ingredients

- 6 cups chicken stock
- 4 cups cooked shredded chicken*
- 2 (15 ounces) cans Great Northern beans, drained
- 2 cups (16 ounces) salsa verde (store-bought or homemade)
- Two teaspoons ground cumin

### Instructions

1. Slow Cooker Method: Add chicken stock, chicken, salsa, and cumin to a slow cooker and stir to combine. Cook for 6-8 hours at low or 3-4 hours at medium, add the beans in the last half hour of cooking.

**Preparation Time** - 5 min

**Servings** - 4

**Macros** - Calories 242, Fat 6g, Saturated Fat 3g, Carbohydrates 5g, Protein 9g

## 33. LEEK LENTIL SOUP

### Ingredients

- Four slices nitrate-free bacon I use Hormel's Natural Choice
- One leek, two cloves garlic
- 3 cups chicken broth
- Red Mill, 1 tsp salt, 1 cup red lentils I use Bob's

### Instructions

2. In medium-high heat, small heat skillet. Chop the bacon roughly and saute until browned for 2-3 minutes, stirring frequently.

3. Remove lentils and garlic and continue to cook for 3 minutes or until the leek starts to soften. Add to a crockpot of 2 thirds.

4. Add the remaining ingredients to the crockpot and stir well. Cook for 2 hours at high heat or for 5-6 hours at low temperature or until the lentils are tender. Enjoy the warmth of crackers with bread or oyster.

**Prep Time** - 10 minutes

**Servings** - 4

**Macros** - Calories 330 Fat 81g Total Fat 9g Saturated Fat 2.5g Total Carbohydrates 33g Protein 23g

## 34. SLOW COOKER BUTTERNUT SQUASH SOUP

### Ingredients

- One large butternut squash, peeled and cut into cubes (approx. 7–8 cups or 1200 g once cubed)
- One white onion, diced (approx. 2 cups, 300 g)
- Four cloves garlic, minced
- 1 cup chopped carrot (approx. 150 g)

- 1/2 tsp cinnamon (optional), 1/2 tsp black pepper, 1/8 tsp ground nutmeg (optional)
- 5–6 cups vegetable stock, 1/2 cup light coconut milk (optional)

## Instructions

1. In a slow cooker, add all the ingredients and cook on high for 4 hours or low for 6-8 hours until the squash is soft and tender.
2. Once cooked, either mix directly with an immersion blender in the slow cooker, or sprinkle carefully in a blender and mix until smooth and creamy. Mix in the milk of the coconut now, if used.
3. If necessary, season with salt and pepper and serve.
4. Residues can be kept for up to 5 days in the fridge or froze for up to 3 months.

**Prep Time** - 10 min

**Servings** - 6 to 8

**Macros** – Calories 159, Fat 5g, Saturated Fat 3g, Carbohydrates 3g, Protein 12g

## 35. CROCKPOT HAM & WHITE BEAN SOUP

### Ingredients

- 6 cups of chicken stock or broth
- 1 lb of dried Great Northern Beans rinsed and sorted through about 1 pound of large ham pieces,
- One medium white onion diced

### Instructions

1. Place and mix all ingredients in the crockpot.

2. Cook for 8 hours at small.
3. Serve warm in the cups.

**Prep time** - 5 min

**Servings** - 4

**Macros** - Calories: 425kcal

## 36. SLOW COOKER CHOCOLATE CHIP COOKIE BARS

### Ingredients

- 2 cups brown sugar tightly packed, 1 cup salted butter melted,
- Three teaspoons vanilla extract
- Two large eggs
- 1 cup chocolate chips any flavor, 2 cups all-purpose flour, 1/4 teaspoon salt

### Instructions

1. Line a slow aluminum foil cooker to create a bowl of foil.
2. Melt butter and brown sugar in a large mixing bowl until smooth. Add extract of vanilla and eggs and stir until smooth. Add salt and flour until well mixed.
3. Pour batter into the bottom of a slow cooker lined with foil. Sprinkle on top of the chocolate chips. Place a towel of paper under the slow cooker's lid.
4. Cook continuously for 2 1/2 to 3 hours before settling in the center. To remove cookies from the slow cooker, use the aluminum foil. Chill before slicing and serving for at least 1 hour.

**Preparation time** - 5 min

Servings - 16

Macros - Calories: 329kcal | Carbohydrates: 46g | Protein: 2g | Fat: 14g | Saturated Fat: 9g

## 37. SLOW COOKER GRANOLA

### Ingredients

- 1 ½ cups (150g) old-fashioned oats
- 2 cups (60g) crisp brown rice cereal
- Two large egg whites, room temperature
- ¼ cup (60mL) honey
- ¼ - ½ cup mix-ins of choice*

### Instructions

1. Coat lightly with nonstick cooking spray the inside of a 5-quarter slow cooker. Line and set aside a wide-rimmed baking sheet with foil.
2. In a large bowl, mix oats and rice cereal. Whisk the egg whites and honey together in a separate bowl. Pour over the cereal mixture of the honey mixture and sprinkle with a spatula until all the cereal is eaten.
3. Transfer the mixture of cereals to the slow cooker
4. Cook the granola for 2 to 2 ½ hours or until crunchy, stirring smoothly every 45 minutes to avoid burning of the nearest granola.
5. Once the granola finishes reach your desired crunchy texture, transfer it to the prepared baking sheet to fully cool before sprinkling with your favorite mix-ins.

**Preparation Time** – 10 mins

**Servings** - 5

Macros – Calories 234, Fat 5g, Saturated Fat 3g, Carbohydrates 6g, Protein 7g

## 38. SLOW COOKER BERRY BREAKFAST QUINOA

### Ingredients

- Two ripe bananas, mashed
- 4 cups of water, 2 cups quinoa, rinsed
- 2 cups fresh or frozen mixed berries (blueberries, strawberries, raspberries, etc.)
- 2 Tbsp maple syrup
- 2 tsp. Vanilla, 1 tsp. Cinnamon, ¼ tsp. salt

### Instructions

1. Spray a three or 4-quart slow cooker with cooking spray then add mashed bananas along with the rest of ingredients, mixing well. Cover and place on low for 5 to 6 hours or on high for 2 to 3 hours.
2. Spoon quinoa into bowls and top with additional fruit or nuts, enjoy!

**Macros** - Serving Size: 1 cup • Calories: 229 • Fat: 2.8 g • Saturated Fat: 0 g • Carbs: 44.2 g • Fiber: 6 g • Protein: 7 g • Sugar: 12.5 g

**Servings** - 8

**Preparation Time** – 15 mins

## 39. SLOW COOKER SPINACH AND MUSHROOM FRITTATA

### Ingredients

- Six eggs, lightly beaten
- Salt and pepper to taste

- Two garlic cloves, minced
- Three mushrooms, sliced
- 1 cup fresh spinach, 1/2 cup – 1 cup shredded cheese

## Instructions

1. Spray an oven-safe dish that fits inside your large slow cooker with non-stick cooking spray.
2. Combine the eggs, salt, and pepper, garlic, mushrooms, spinach in the dish. Sprinkle the top with cheese.
3. Put the dish in the slow cooker's center.
4. Slice and serve.

**Preparation Time** - 10

**Macros** - Calories 109, Fat 6g, Saturated Fat 2g, Carbohydrates 4g, Protein 8g

**Servings** - 6

## 40. SLOW COOKER APPLE CINNAMON OATMEAL

### Ingredients

- 3 cups plain unsweetened almond milk
- 3 cups of water
- 1.5 cups steel-cut oats, 1/3 cup maple syrup
- Two teaspoons ground cinnamon, 1/8 teaspoon salt
- Two large apples, shredded

## Instructions

1. In a slow cooker, add oats, almond milk, water, maple syrup, cinnamon and salt, and mix.
2. Cover and cook for about 6-8 hours at low or 3-4 at high. If you can, we recommend that you stir all that often.
3. When fully cooked, cut two large apples and shred them. Add and mix in the slow cooker— cook for another 30 minutes.
4. Serve with nut butter, cinnamon, and shredded apple.

**Servings** - 6

**Macros** - Size: 1/6 Calories: 260, Sugar: 16g, Sodium: 112g, Fat: 4g, Carbohydrates: 49g, Fiber: 8g, Protein: 8g

**Preparation Time** - 10 min

# KETO PORK RECIPES

## 41. KETO PORK CARNITAS WITH LETTUCE WRAPS

**Ingredients:** olive oil, dried oregano, lime juice, pork shoulder, chicken broth, lettuce leaves, cumin powder, chili powder, paprika, onion, garlic, lime wedges, flat-leaf parsley, salt, pepper.

### Instructions

1. In a small bowl, mix chili powder, dried oregano, cumin salt ground, and pepper.
2. Season the pork on all sides and put in your slow cooker the seasoned pork.
3. Add lime juice, garlic, chopped onions, orange juice.
4. Cook for 8 hours at low or 4-5 hours at medium.
5. Use two forks to shred the meat— no need for this step to take the pork out of the slow cooker.
6. Serve with cilantro, chopped red onion, and sour cream (optional) on Bibb lettuce.

**Preparation Time** – 10 mins

**Servings** - 12

**Macros** - Calories 62 kcal, Fat 3.1g, Net carbs 1.3g, Protein 7g

## 42. KETO SLOW COOKER ASIAN PORK RIBS

**Ingredients:** rack of baby back pork rib, garlic paste, ginger paste, onion, chicken broth, gluten-free tamari sauce or coconut aminos, Chinese five-spice seasoning, green onions.

### Instructions

1. Put the ribs of pork in a slow cooker. The frame may need to be halved to fit it.
2. Add the onions, paste of garlic, a paste of ginger, and broth of chicken. If the ribs are not fully covered, add a little bit more broth before covered.
3. Cook for 3 hours and cover the ingredients at low.
4. To stay warm, cut the ribs and cover them with foil. Set aside.
5. Use a blender to blitz well, then add the 5-spice tamari and Chinese. Reduce the mixture too thick and jammy over moderately high heat.
6. Move the onions and stock to a clean pan on the stove from the slow cooker.
7. To taste the marinade, add a pinch of erythritol, and if you think it would benefit with a little sugar.
8. Brush the marinade with sliced green onions over the hot ribs.

**Preparation Time** – 20 mins

**Servings** – 2

**Macros** – Calories 482 kcal, Fats 38g, Net Carbs 4g, Protein 25g, Carbohydrates 5g, Fibre 1g

## 43. KETO SLOW COOKER LETTUCE WRAPS KALUA PORK

**Ingredients**: liquid smoke, sea salt, tomatoes, pork butt or pork shoulder, bell pepper, olive oil, apple cider vinegar, iceberg lettuce.

## Instructions

1. Mix the salt with the liquid smoke.
2. Use a knife to make some small holes in the pork to help get the flavor in.
3. Stroke the salt mixture of liquid smoke into the food.
4. Place in your slow cooker until the meat is very tender and cook at low for 8 hours.
5. Mix the tomatoes, bell pepper, olive oil, and vinegar to make the salsa.
6. Chop the pork finely and enjoy a sauce scoop in lettuce wraps.

**Preparation Time** – 5 mins

**Servings** – 10

**Macros** - Calories 394 kcal, Fats 28g, Net Carbs 1g, Protein 32g, Carbohydrates 2g, Fibre 1g

## 44. KETO CROCKPOT PORK SHANKS WITH GRAVY

**Ingredients:** olive oil, onions, garlic cloves, lemon juice, pork shanks (on the bone), chicken broth, dried bay leaves, dijon mustard, ghee.

## Instruction

1. Heat a tsp of olive oil in a frying pan until the skin is browned. Remove and set aside.
2. Apply the second tablespoon of olive oil to the same pan and add the onions and garlic until the onions caramelize. Deglaze the pan with the

lemon juice and scrape off any stuck pieces.
3. Place the shanks in a crockpot and pour the cooked onion.
4. Take the shanks from the crockpot and place them on a roasting tray. Preheat the oven to the full.
5. Place the tray on the bottom rack once the oven is heated and cook until the skin is crisping and puffing up. Remove before serving and allow to rest.
6. Make gravy in the meantime. Spoon all the crockpot cooking juices and onions into a large saucepan on the stovetop.
7. Serve the shanks with your favorite greens and gravy.

**Preparation Time** – 10 min

**Servings** – 4

**Macros** - Calories 355 kcal, Fats 30g, Net Carbs 3g, Protein 13g, Carbohydrates 7g, Fibre 1g

## 45. KETO CROCKPOT PORK CHOPS

**Ingredients:** pork chops, onion, mushrooms, olive oil, warm beef or chicken broth, gluten-free, tamari sauce, salt, freshly ground black pepper, chives.

## Instructions

1. In a bowl, mix the rosemary, curry powder, chives, fennel seed, cumin, salt, thyme, and 1/2 of the olive oil.
2. Rub the spice mixture with the pork chops to coat the meat evenly.
3. In the slow cooker, pour the remaining olive oil. Add the meat to the slow cooker and cook on high for

4 hours, medium for 6 hours, or low for 8 hours.

**Preparation Time** – 5 min

**Servings** – 8

**Macros** - Calories 247 kcal, Fats 15g, Net Carbs 3g, Protein 24g, Carbohydrates 1g,

# 46. CROCKPOT PORK

**Ingredients**: pork shoulder, salt, ginger powder, Szechuan, peppercorns.

**Instructions**

1. Cut the pork into the cooker slowly.
2. Use the cajun seasoning to cover the meat and place it in the slow cooker.
3. Place the 1/2 cup of water in the slow cooker base.
4. Cook at low for 10 hours.
5. Once the pork has been shredded, add salt to taste.

**Preparation Time** – 5 min

**Servings** – 6 to 8

**Macros** - Calories 247 kcal, Fats 15g, Net Carbs 3g, Protein 24g, Carbohydrates 1g,

# 47. CROCKPOT PULLED PORK CHILI

**Ingredients**: pork roast, garlic cloves, cayenne pepper, red pepper flakes, salt, yellow onions, red bell pepper, yellow bell pepper, hot sauce, smoked paprika, garlic powder, chili powder, cumin, fire-roasted tomatoes, tomato sauce, avocado, green onions.

**Instructions**

1. To start slow cooking, add all the ingredients.

2. Cover and cook 7-9 hours on a low.
3. Remove and shred the pork roast with the forks.
4. Return to cooker slowly and combine to stir.
5. Serve with cheese and sour cream or merely plain as desired!

**Preparation Time** – 10 min

**Servings** – 6

**Macros** - Calories 301 kcal, Fats 7g, Net Carbs 2g, Protein 26g, Carbohydrates 30g,

# 48. KETO PULLED PORK

**Ingredients:** chili powder, salt, cinnamon, granulated sweetener, pork shoulder, onion, garlic, chicken stock, liquid smoke, paprika, garlic powder, pepper, cumin, keto-friendly BBQ sauce.

**Instruction**

1. Place all the seasonings in a small bowl.
2. Place the pork roast with the seasoned pasta in your slow cooker, skin side down, smother the roast completely.
3. Turn the roast to face the side of the skin. In the slow cooker, add the vinegar by pouring it to the side, no over the roast.
4. Place the lid and cook the roast on low or 8-9 hours on high for 10-12 hours.
5. Shred the roast when finished and put the meat back in the juice for 10-15 minutes to rest. The pulled pork is going to absorb the juice flavors.

**Preparation Time** – 5 min

**Servings** – 6 to 8

Macros - Calories 181 kcal, Fats 8.3g, Net Carbs 0.1g, Protein 24.7g, Carbohydrates 0.1g, fiber 0.05

## 49. SLOW COOKER PORK STEW OYSTER MUSHROOMS

**Ingredients:** coconut oil, onion, garlic, pork loin, nutmeg, broth, wine vinegar, oyster mushrooms, Himalayan salt, black pepper, oregano, dried, mustard, full-fat coconut milk, ghee, capers.

### Instructions

Add medium-high heat oil to a large pan, add the onion and cook for 4-5 minutes, stirring frequently. Sprinkle with paprika, garlic, salt, and pepper pork chops.

Add mushrooms and cook 3-4 minutes more.

In the slow cooker, add mushrooms and mixture of onions, chicken broth, and thyme sprigs to the pork chops.

**Preparation Time –** 10 min

**Servings –** 4

**Macros -** Calories 611 kcal, Fats 33g, Net Carbs 19g, Protein 63g, Carbohydrates 20g, fiber 7g

## 50. SLOW COOKER PORK TACOS RECIPE

**Ingredients:** pork butt/shoulder, oregano, red pepper flakes, ground cloves, chili powder, kosher salt, cumin, stock or broth, bay leaf.

### Instructions

1. Combine the red pepper flakes in a bowl with sugar, cumin, oregano, chili powder, and cloves.
2. Rub the spice mixture on all sides of the pork with your hands.
3. Remove the string and put it on a clean plate around the pork.
4. Place the pork with the bay leaf and 1/2 cup broth or stock in a slow cooker. Set for 8 hours at low.
5. After removing it from the liquid, place it on a cutting board. Take two forks and shred the meat.

**Preparation Time –** 5 min

**Servings –** 10

**Macros -** Calories 190 kcal, Fats 9g, Net Carbs 3g, Protein 24g, Carbohydrates 1g,

## 51. EASY COLLARD GREENS WITH BACON

**Ingredients:** bacon, onion, collard greens, pork or chicken stock, bacon fat or coconut oil, onion, garlic, apple cider vinegar.

### Instructions

1. Heat a high-sided pan with bacon fat or coconut oil while the bacon is cooking. Dice the onion over low-medium heat and add to the pan. Saute for about 5 minutes until soft. Add the garlic until fragrant for a minute, then add about half of the greens of the collar.
2. Before adding the remaining collard greens to the pan, let the collard greens wilt.
3. When done, remove the bacon on a towel-lined sheet of paper. Wait for a few minutes, then cut into small

pieces. Combine the bacon with the wild greens mixture, then add in the apple cider vinegar.

4. Add the wilted collard greens mixture to a large slow cooker, along with 2 cups of stock. Cover them and cook on low for 5 – 6 hours.

**Preparation Time** – 15 min

**Servings** – 4

**Macros** - Calories 72.9 kcal, Fats 4.5g, Protein 3.1g, Carbohydrates 6.8g, fiber 2.4g

# 52. CROCKPOT LUAU PORK WITH CAULI RICE

**Ingredients**: pork roast, bacon, garlic, hickory liquid smoke, cauliflower, Hawaiian black lava sea salt chicken broth, garlic powder, sea salt.

## Instructions

1. Set the crockpot to high setting and line the crockpot bottom with the slices of the raw bacon. Sprinkle the hairy garlic over the bacon top.
2. When needed, slice a little fat off the bottom of a roast.
3. Punch and stab holes all over and through the roast with a sharp knife.
4. Pour 1 1/2 to 2 tbsp of black lava sea salt into a small pinch bowl and use your fingers to rub salt throughout the roast (will be a charcoal mess on your hands, but it is easy to wash away).
5. Place roast in the crockpot, fat side down. Add optional liquid smoke and cover crockpot over the top of the roast. Cook for 4 to 6 hours at high (longer bone-in roasting time), then for 2 hours at low. Could also

cook for 8 hours to 10 hours at low (if your roast has a bone in it, it will take 8 to 10 hours). Once the time for cooking is up, take a fork and remove the roast in the crockpot (if done, it should quickly fall apart). Stir in the crockpot and cover shredded pork and bacon. Cook 30 minutes on low.

6. If you decide to make the rice of cauliflower, now is the time to start making it. Steam cauliflower in the food processor for 20 minutes or microwave for 5 minutes, but slightly cooled cauliflower and add chicken broth, garlic, and sea salt.
7. Process until the texture of the rice is created.
8. Place a cauli rice scoop on a plate and add a shredded luau pork scoop.
9. Serve and make the most of it.

**Preparation Time** – 9 min

**Servings** – 10

**Macros** - Calories 182 kcal, Fats 13g, Net Carbs 3g, Protein 14g, Carbohydrates 2g, Fiber 0.9g

# 53. CROCKPOT CHILI VERDE

**Ingredients:** butter, cilantro, pork stewing meat or chicken, salsa verde, garlic, sea salt, cilantro.

## Instructions

1. Heat the oil in a Dutch oven with medium heat. Cook and stir until it is fragrant, add the onion and garlic. Add the pork and cook until the outside is browned. Add the green salsa, jalapeno peppers, and tomatoes in a slow cooker, and move the beef, onions, and garlic.

2. Cover and cook on High for 3 hours. Reduce setting to low and add 4 to 5 hours of cooking.

**Servings** - 12

**Preparation Time** - 30 min

**Macros** - 265 calories; 12.4 g fat; 12.1 g carbohydrates; 22.5 g protein; 64 mg

## 54. CROCKPOT PORK LOIN

**Ingredients:** onions, beef/chicken stock, salt, pepper, pork loin

**Instructions**

1. Pour over the pork with the sauce. Close the cooker gradually.
2. Pork loin-Cook 4 to 5 hours on LOW.
3. Pork Shoulder-Cook for 10 hours on LOW (oven, IP, and pressure cooker note 6).
4. Remove pork from a serving plate and cover with foil loosely (10-20 minutes rest).
5. Pour all the juices into a large saucepan in a slow cooker. Attach the mixture of cornflour steam, blend.
6. Thickened sauce: Simmer for 5 minutes at medium-high or until it reduces to a consistency of syrup (Note 2).
7. In thick slices of pork (1.5-2 cm/3/5-4/5 "thick). Serve with the Honey Butter Sauce PLENTY!

**Preparation Time** - 10 min

**Servings** - 8

**Macros** - Calories: 561kcal Carbohydrates: 28g Protein: 56g Fat: 23g Saturated Fat: 11g

## 55. CROCKPOT KALUA PIG

**Ingredients**: pork shoulder, sea salt, liquid smoke.

**Instructions**

Pierce pork with a carving fork throughout. Rub salt over the meat and then smoke liquid. In a slow cooker, put the roast.

Cover and cook for 16 to 20 hours on low, turning once during the cooking time.

Remove meat from slow cooking and shredding, adding drippings to moisturize as needed.

**Preparation Time** -10

**Servings** - 12

**Macros** - 243 calories; 14.7 g fat; 0 g carbohydrates; 25.9 g protein

## 56. SLOW COOKER ITALIAN PORK ROAST

**Ingredients**: pork roast, Penzeys Italian Herb Mix, garlic, salt.

**Instructions**

1. Pat the dry roast of pork with towels of paper. Use a small sharp knife to make pork slits and insert the garlic slivers in the slits.
2. Use your hands to smash the leaves and mix them with the salt in a small bowl. Rub the mixture into the nooks and crannies throughout the pork roast.
3. In the slow cooker, put the pork roast and cook at low for 14 to 16 hours. The slow cooker's pan will fill with liquid as the pork roasts.

4. It's fall-apart tender when the meat is finished roasting. You can shred it with forks, mix the crusty bits with the inside, tender bits, or break it into chunks of serving size. Either way, it's crazy-good. Recall the juice that you put in the refrigerator? Now you can skim off the excess fat quickly, reheat the juice in a pot on the stove, and use it as a cooked meat sauce.

**Preparation Time** - 10 min

**Servings** – 4

**Macros**
Calories 130, Fat 4g, Carbohydrates 3g
Fiber 1g, Protein 20g

## 57. NEW MEXICO CARNE ADOVADA

**Ingredients:** pork shoulder, New Mexican chilies, onion, garlic, Mexican oregano, ground cumin, ground coriander, kosher salt, chicken or beef stock, apple cider vinegar.

**Instructions**

1. Remove from the red chiles the stems and seeds. Cut into 1 "strips.
2. Add olive oil over medium heat to a large saucepan. Mix in chilies, onion, and garlic. Saute for 5 to 10 minutes until fragrant. Pour in milk, salt, and oregano, stirring well. Bring to boil, cover, and reduce heat to a simmer for 10 minutes.
3. Move chili mixture to a blender, in batches if needed, and mix until smooth.

**Preparation Time** - 60 mins

**Servings** 4

**Macros** - 704 Calories 38g Fat 26gCarbs 63g Protein

## 58. PULLED PORK TACO SALAD

**Ingredients:** pulled pork, red bell pepper, onion, romaine lettuce, pico de gallo, guacamole, primal palate Adobo seasoning, avocado oil, Tessemae's Southwest Ranch, or dressing of choice.

**Instructions**

1. Heat over medium-high heat a casserole and add to the avocado oil.
2. Add the pepper when the oil is hot, add the peppers and onions sliced, and the seasoning with adobo.
3. Cut the onions and peppers until they are relatively soft but not mushy.
4. Place shredded lettuce with pulled pork, guacamole, Gallo pico, and onion and pepper mixture in a bowl and top.
5. Topdressing or dressing of choice for Tessemae's Southwest Ranch.

**Preparation Time** - 10 mins

**Servings** 4

**Macros** - 934 Calories, 83g Carbs

(70g net carbs), 48g Fat, 41g Protein

## 59. SLOW COOKER COCONUT CURRY PORK

**Ingredients:** pork stew meat, onions, garlic, ginger, tomatoes, coconut milk, curry powder, ground cumin, turmeric, salt bone broth, parsley, cauliflower rice.

## Instruction

1. Heat the oil in a big skillet. Spice the salt and peppered pork and add half of the pork to the skillet and brown over moderately high heat for about 12 minutes. Put the pork in the slow cooker. Repeat the rest of the pork.

2. Pour off the fat in the skillet except for two teaspoons. Add the onion, curry, cumin, garlic, ginger, and turmeric and cook until the onion is softened for about 5 minutes. Scrape into the slow cooker the mixture. Add the coconut milk, tomatoes and their juices, stock cover, and cook for 4 hours on high. Spoon off much fat as possible from the stew's surface. Serve stew over rice in large bowls with cilantro and scallions Serve stew over rice in large bowls with cilantro and scallions.

**Preparation Time** - 15 mins

**Servings** - 4

**Macros** - Calories457, Fat 32.0 g, Saturated 15.9 g Carbs21.9 g Fiber 2.6 g Sugars1.7 g Protein 22.1 g

## 60. KETO SLOW COOKER BRISKET CHILI

### Ingredient

Beef brisket, olive oil, onion, green bell pepper, ground cumin, garlic, mushrooms, chili powder, beef stock, tomatoes, salt, ground black pepper, flat-leaf parsley.

### Instructions

1. Add 2 Tablespoons of olive oil in a large saucepan. Brown and set aside the brisket on all sides.
2. Add the remaining 2 Tablespoons of olive oil and sauté the onions, garlic, mushrooms, green bell pepper, and Jalapeño pepper. Also, add cumin powder and chili powder.
3. Layer the brisket with sautéed vegetables in a slow cooker. Remove the beef broth and the tomatoes. Cover and cook for 6 hours on medium, turning the brisket periodically.
4. In the slow cooker, shred the meat and cook for another hour.
5. Serve over mashed cauliflower or cauliflower rice with salt and freshly ground black pepper.

**Servings** - 6

**Prep TIme** - 15 min

**Macros**Calories: 43, Sugar: 4g, Fat: 3g Carbohydrates: 8g Fiber: 2g Protein: 22 g

## 61. KETO CROCKPOT BEEF STROGANOFF

### Ingredient

Beef roast, onion, chicken bone broth, garlic, parsley, white mushrooms, Kettle & Fire Mushroom, salt, pepper, cucumber, coconut milk/cream, Dijon mustard, salt, parsley.

### Instructions

1. In a slow cooker/crockpot, place the beef, onion, garlic, mushrooms, beef broth, black pepper, and salt and cook at a low temperature. Six to eight hours.
2. Stir in the slow cooker dish, the coconut cream, Dijon mustard, salt to taste after the beef has been cooked.
3. Place the noodles of the cucumber in a bowl. Top with the stroganoff beef. Garnish with the parsley that remains.

**Servings** - 6

**Prep Time** - 10 mins

**Macros** - Serving Size: 1 bowl Calories: 462 Sugar: 2g Saturated Fat: 36g Carbohydrates: 4g Fiber: 1 g Protein: 26 g

## 62. EASY SLOW COOKER KETO POT ROAST

### Ingredient

Beef roast stalks of celery, Italian seasoning, carrot, onion, garlic cloves, beef broth.

### Instruction

1. Place all in the slow cooker and cook until the beef is tender for 8 hours.

**Servings** - 8

**Prep Time** - 10 mins

**Macros**      - Calories: 468 Sugar: 1      g
Fat:36g Carbohydrates: 3g Fiber: 1g Protein: 29 g

## 63. KETO INSTANT POT BEEF STEW

### Ingredient

Beef stew chunks, gluten-free tamari sauce or coconut aminos, carrots, tomatoes, onion, beef broth, mushrooms (optional), parsley.

### Instruction

1. Apply to your Instant Pot or pressure cooker all the ingredients.
2. Securely close the lid and press on your Instant Pot with the Stew option. It should be cooked for about an hour.
3. After depressurizing, carefully open the lid.
4. Pour over chopped parsley into bowls and top.

**Servings** - 6

**Prep time** - 5

**Macros** - Calories: 437 Sugar: 2gFat: 32 g Carbohydrates: 6 g Fiber: 2 g Protein: 28 g

## 64. KETO SLOW-COOKED SHREDDED BEEF

### Ingredient

Beef roast, olive oil, vinegar, beef broth, Tomato Sauce, red & green onions, garlic cloves, fresh ginger, gluten-free tamari sauce, or coconut aminos, erythritol, iceberg lettuce leaves.

### Instructions

1. Halve the grain with the beef roast. (Two pieces means that the beef is completely submerged in the slow cooker stock. This is optional but recommended.)
2. In a large pan, heat one tablespoon of olive oil and cook the beef on all sides until dark and golden. Delete it and put it aside.
3. Heat the second tablespoon of olive oil in the same pan and cook the onions, garlic, and ginger until all the onions have softened and caramelized.
4. Deglaze the pan with the vinegar for the red wine. When finished, add in the beef broth for a minute to warm up.
5. Tip the whole mixture into a slow cooker and add the piece(s) of brown beef for 3 hours— cover and cook. Remove the beef after 3 hours and set aside to rest, covered with foil.
6. Pour the remaining mixture into a clean pan on the stove from the slow cooker. Attach the sauce of tomatoes and tamari. Reduce the mixture to one-third of the original yield over moderately high water, stirring occasionally. Remove the erythritol.
7. Meanwhile, use two forks to shred after the beef has rested for at least 10 minutes. In the hot sauce, add the pulled beef and stir well to mix.
8. In the lettuce leaves, serve the shredded beef and garnish with the onions. Wrap the lettuce around and enjoy the shredded beef as a healthy Keto wrap!

**Servings** - 8

**Prep time** - 20

**Macros** - Calories: 221 Sugar: 2g Fat: 17 g Carbohydrates: 4 g Fiber: 1 g Protein: 11 g

# 65. KETO CROCKPOT SPAGHETTI AND PESTO MEATBALLS

## Ingredient

Ground beef, olive oil, beef broth, pine nuts, garlic cloves, lemon zest and juice, basil leaves, salt, pepper, zucchinis, ground black pepper.

## Instructions

1. Make the pesto by mixing all the ingredients of pesto. To serve with, set aside 1/2.
2. Combine ground beef and basil pesto with the other half and form 1oz/30 g small balls in size.
3. Heat the olive oil and fry the balls of meat (in batches) until all brown. Place the beef broth in the slow cooker.
4. Cover and cook for 2 hours, now and then spoon the broth over the meatballs.
5. With the remainder of the pesto, throw the zucchini noodles.
6. Season to taste with meatballs on top with salt and freshly ground black pepper.

**Prep time** 15 min

**Servings** 2

**Macros** Calories: 522 Sugar: 1g Fat: 48g Carbohydrates: 3 g Fiber: 1 g Protein: 20 g

# 66. SIMPLE BONE BROTH

## Ingredients

Bones, water, apple cider vinegar.

## Instructions

1. In a large pan or stock, put the olive oil. Add the onions, celery, leek, and mushrooms once the oil gets cold. Cook over moderate heat to ensure that the vegetables are not burned or caramelized.
2. Add the fish bones and cold water once the onions have softened. Bring the mixture to a cooler and partly cover with a lid — cook over low-moderate heat for 1 hour.
3. Use cheesecloth or fine-mesh sieve to strain the broth, then season with salt and ground white pepper.
4. When you like it on your own, serve warm, and chives garnished.

**Prep Time** - 10 mins

**Servings** - 4

**Macros** - Calories: 61 Sugar: 3 g Fat: 4 g Carbohydrates: 7 g Fiber: 1 g Protein: 1 g

# 67. SLOW COOKER ASIAN POT ROAST

## Ingredient

Beef round roast, coconut aminos, garlic powder, beef broth, salt, onion powder or minced onion dried or fresh cilantro leaves, star of anise, Szechuan peppercorns.

## Instruction

1. Coat the roast with black pepper, garlic powder, and mustard powder while the skillet is heating up. Add

the roast on both sides of the skillet and brown (about 5 minutes per side).

2. From the skillet, remove the roast and add to the crockpot. Pour over the remaining roast ingredients—cover and cook for 6-8 hours at low.
3. Serve over rice and sauté.

**Prep time** - 15 mins

**Servings** - 8

**Macros** - Calories 580, Fat 34g, Saturated Fat 15g, Carbohydrates 12g, Fiber 1g, Sugar 9g, Protein 57g

# 68. PALEO CROCKPOT OXTAIL WITH MUSTARD GRAVY

## Ingredients

Oxtail, chicken broth, Dijon mustard, salt.

## Instructions

1. In the crockpot, place the oxtail and chicken broth and cook for 10 hours at low. The meat and broth can then be stored in the fridge until you are ready to eat it.
2. Cook the oxtail (meat can fall off) in a stockpot at low heat with what's left of the broth to reduce the broth to the gravy when you're ready to eat. I suggest that you do this in lots.
3. Stir in the mustard when the broth boils down and becomes thinner (such as a thin gravy consistency) (add one tablespoon at a time to see how good you like the mustard flavor).
4. Serve and add salt to taste.

**Prep Time** - 5mins

**Servings** - 4 to 6

**Macros** - 433 calories; 25.1 g fat; 5 g carbohydrates; 46.8 g protein; 171 mg cholesterol; 1848 mg sodium.

# 69. PALEO SLOW COOKER OXTAIL STEW

## Ingredients

Oxtail, water, tomatoes, garlic, paprika, salt.

## Instructions

1. Place the oxtail with the water in the slow cooker and cook for 10 hours at low heat (the meat should be very tender and fall apart at the end).
2. To make the stew when you're ready to eat, add the tomatoes, garlic, and spices to the oxtail saucepan (if necessary, you can cook it in several lots) and stew for 10-15 minutes.
3. Apply to taste the oil.

**Prep time** - 5 mins

**Servings** - 4

**Macros** - Calories 439 Fat 19g Saturated Fat 7g Carbohydrates 10g Fiber 3g Sugar 3g Protein 53g

# 70. PALEO ROPA VIEJA RECIPE

## Ingredient

Flank steak, coconut oil, olive oil, peppers, onion flakes (or onion powder), garlic powder, white wine vinegar, sea salt, cilantro, parsley, garlic, tomato paste, oregano, cumin powder.

## Instructions

1. Cut the steak (against the grain) into two-inch-wide strips.
2. In a large frying pan, put one tablespoon of coconut oil and turn the heat to medium. Pan sear half of the steak strips on the flank–leave on each side in the frying pan for 2-3 minutes. Continue with the other half of the pieces of the flank steak.
3. Put in the slow cooker all the ingredients and the steak strips of the seared flank.
4. Make sure all the ingredients are combined with your mouth.
5. At low heat level, set the slow cooker and cook for 6 hours.
6. Shred the steak on the flank and mix it before feeding.

**Prep TIme** - 20 mins

**Servings** - 6 to 8

**Macros** - 36.5g Protein | 16.8g Carbs | 20g Fat | 4.5g Fiber | 400 Calories

## 71. SLOW-COOKED CORNED BEEF BRISKET AND ROASTED CABBAGE

### Ingredient

Corned beef brisket, onion, carrot, green cabbage, celery stalk, chicken or beef stock, avocado oil, salt, pepper.

### Instruction

1. Use a slow cooker with corned beef brisket and spices.
2. Pour over brisket 4 cups or enough water to cover the whole roast.
3. Remove celery, carrots, and onions. Cover and cook steadily for 6 to 8 hours at low or 4 to 5 hours at high.

4. Apply the last half hour of cooking time to the cabbage, cover, and continue cooking for the remaining 30 minutes.
5. Remove vegetables and chicken from the crockpot with a slotted spoon to remove excess liquid.
6. Cut and cut the corned beef against the grain. Honor. Serve.

**Prep time** - 6 mins

**Servings** - 8

**Macros** - Serving: 6ounces | Calories: 158kcal | Carbohydrates: 4g | Protein: 27g | Fat: 6g | Saturated Fat: 3g | Fiber: 1g

## 72. SLOW COOKER BEEF STROGANOFF

### Ingredient

Beef stew meat, salt, pepper, paprika, thyme, onion powder, garlic powder, mushrooms, onion, coconut cream, red wine vinegar.

### Instructions

1. In a pan, melt olive oil. Cook beef in small quantities of salt and pepper and brown in olive oil. Deglaze the red wine casserole and add it to the slow cooker.
2. In a 6qt slow cooker, put beef, garlic powder, onions, dijon, Worcestershire, mushrooms, and 1 1/2 cups of broth.
3. Cook for 4-5 hours or 7-8 hours or as long as the beef is soft.
4. Combine the remaining cornstarch broth and whisk in the slow cooker. Cover the lid and cook for 15 minutes or until thickened.

5. Cut the sour cream. Serve over the noodles of the egg.

**Prep Time** - 20 mins

**Servings** - 8

**Macros** - Calories: 568, Fat: 32g, Saturated Fat: 13g, Carbohydrates: 38g, Fiber: 2g, Sugar: 3g, Protein: 29g,

## 73. SPICY BEEF CURRY

### Ingredient

Beef chuck, white onion, whole fat coconut milk, salt, curry powder, garlic, ginger, chili sauce.

### Instructions

1. Place the ingredients of beef and marinade in a medium-sized bowl and mix until all is combined. I like using my hands to rub the meat with yogurt. Cover with plastic wrap and put for 1-2 hours (or overnight) in the fridge to marinate.

2. Place a large frying pan over high heat (or the inside of your slow-cooker if it can be used on the hob) and spray with the fry light. Attach the beef and cook until sealed for 5-6 minutes. When you prepare, you'll probably notice watery liquid coming out of the meat and marinade. Drain most of it (otherwise, you're just going to cook the meat). Nonetheless, leaving a little in there is perfect.

3. Once the beef has been sewn, add the onion and turn the heat to high. Remove and cook until the onion begins to soften for 4-5 minutes.

4. Apply chilies, garlic, and ginger to the coriander, cumin, cardamom, turmeric, garam masala, black pepper. Cook for 3-4 minutes, stirring several times until the scent of the spices starts to emerge.

5. Attach tomato paste, stock, chopped tomatoes, and juice of a lemon. Bring to a simmer, then switch to your slow cooker and cook for 3-4 hours at high or 5-6 hours at low.

6. When cooked, if necessary, test and add salt and pepper. Use some freshly chopped coriander to serve over beans.

**Prep Time** - 15 mins

**Servings** - 6

**Macros** - Calories 224 Fat 3.7g Saturated Fat 1.2g Carbohydrates 18.5g Fiber 2.2g Sugar 6.9g Protein 29.7g

## 74. BACON CABBAGE CHUCK BEEF STEW

### Ingredient

Bacon, chuck roast, Celtic sea salt, black pepper, red onions, garlic, cabbage, thyme, beef bone broth.

### Instructions

1. Attach bacon slices to the bottom, onion slices and garlic, chuck roast, cabbage slices, thyme, broth, attach a few pinches of sea salt and a generous quantity of freshly ground black pepper to your slow cooker in the following order.

2. Cook for 7 hours at small.

3. Serve all flatbread crackers [ 7 g carb] in 1thin cups.

**Prep time** - 10 mins

**Servings** - 4 to 6

**Macros** - Calories: 594.4 Total Fat: 38.5 g Total Carbs: 5.1 g Dietary Fiber: 1.5 g Protein: 52.0 g

## 75. SLOW COOKER MIDDLE EASTERN BEEF

### Ingredients

Beef brisket, Sea salt, pepper, fennel seeds, whole cloves, whole peppercorns, cumin powder, cardamom powder, ground cinnamon, tomato paste, onion, bone broth, coconut vinegar or apple cider vinegar

### Instructions

1. Heat the oven up to 300 ° F/150 ° C.
2. Mix the spices, salt, and pepper in a small bowl.
3. Press the beef into a shallow casserole dish or roasting pan with about 1½ tablespoons of the spice mixture to coat it. Place the remaining spice mix for your next brisket in a small jar.
4. Add the garlic, onion, and pour over the stock (the meat should be covered or nearly covered).
5. Cover tightly wrapped with a cap or foil to seal.
6. Cook for about 2 hours, transform the meat and cook for 2-3 hours (total cooking time of 4-5 hours). When the beef quickly falls apart when it is pulled at, it is fried.
7. Remove the cover or foil and turn the oven to 200 ° C. Take the meat apart and cook to caramelize and thicken the sauce for about 30 minutes.
8. Combine all the ingredients of the tahini sauce to make your tahini

sauce. Apply the tablespoon of water until you have a slightly runny sauce that can be poured over the food.

**Prep Time** - 10 mins

**Servings** - 4

**Macros** - Calories: 494 Total Fat: 28.5 g Total Carbs: 4.1 g Dietary Fiber: 1.5 g Protein: 42.0 g

## 76. NOSE TO TAIL SLOW COOKER BEEF RENDANG

### Ingredients

Desiccated coconut, dried birds eye chilies, ground cumin, ground coriander, turmeric powder, salt, water, garlic, shallots, red chilies, coconut oil, kafir lime leaves, lemongrass, coconut cream, cinnamon stick, tamarind paste, stevia liquid, beef cheek, oxtail, cilantro leaves.

### Instructions

1. Chop the ingredients of the spice paste and then combine them in a food processor until they are finished.
2. In a stew pot heat the oil, add the paste of spice, cinnamon, cloves, star anise, and cardamom, and stir-fry until aromatic. Attach the lemongrass and the beef and cook for 1 minute. Add coconut milk, tamarind juice, water, and simmer over medium heat, frequently stirring until the meat is nearly cooked. Remove the leaves of kaffir lime, kerisik (toasted coconut), sugar or palm sugar, and mix well with the food.
3. Reduce heat to a minimum, cover the lid and cook for 1 to 1 1/2 hours

or until the meat has dried up. Apply to taste more salt and sugar. Serve with steamed rice right away and save for overnight.

**Prep Time** - 15 mins

**Servings** - 4

**Macros** - Calories 416 Fat 52g Saturated Fat 24g Carbohydrates 20g Fiber 4g Sugar 9g Protein 36g

# 77. SLOW COOKER MEXICAN BEEF STEW

## Ingredients

Beef stew meat, red onion, garlic, beefsteak tomatoes, green chilies, chili powder, oregano, cumin, Sea salt, pepper, broth, water.

## Instructions

1. Line a 5-to6-quarter slow cooker with a Slow Cooker Liner from Reynolds(R).
2. Coat the flour with the meat. Cook and stir beef about 5 minutes or until browned in a large skillet in hot oil over medium-high heat.
3. In the prepared slow cooker liner, put the beans, carrots, onion, and garlic. Top on the beef. Add tomatoes, broth, ground chili, cumin, salt, and pepper.
4. Cover and cook for 7 hours or until fork-tender is the beef.
5. Gently stir the corn with a rubber spatula. Cover and cook for another 10 minutes or until warm. Serve with avocado, coriander, and crushed red pepper if desired.

**Prep Time** - 20 mins

**Servings** - 6

**Macros** - 272 calories; 8.7 g fat; 27 g carbohydrates; 21.9 g protein; 40 mg cholesterol; 646 mg sodium.

# 78. MEATY PALEO CHILI

## Ingredients

Ground, chicken sausages, chili powder, cumin, dried oregano, cinnamon, tomatoes, tomato paste, onions, Anaheim peppers, poblano pepper, green olives, garlic, salt, pepper.

## Instructions

1. Place over the medium-high place a large stockpot. In the hot pan, crumble the ground chuck and sausage and cook until browned evenly. Drain the excess fat away.
2. Cook the bacon in another pan until it is crispy. Apply to the stockpot and crumble. Cook the chopped onion and pepper for about 5 minutes or until the onions are translucent in the bacon drippings. Attach to the store.
3. Add tomatoes, tomato paste and beef stock to the stockpot. Season with garlic, oregano, cumin, pepper, basil, ginger, onion powder, salt, pepper, and cayenneStir in the mixture, then cover and simmer at low heat for at least 2 hours, stirring occasionally.
4. Taste and change salt, pepper, and other spices as needed after 2 hours. The longer the simmers of chili, the better it tastes.
5. Remove from heat and drink, or cold, and serve the next day. Serve

with onions and crumbled bacon or any of your favorite chili toppings!

**Prep Time** - 20 mins

**Servings** - 8

**Macros**- Calories 321 Fat 14g Carbohydrates 7g Sugar 4g Protein 35g

# 79. SPAGHETTI SQUASH AND MEATBALLS IN MARINARA SAUCE

## Ingredients

Ground beef, ground pork, eggs, almond flour, onion, garlic powder, oregano, smoked paprika, basil, salt, pepper, marinara sauce, squash.

## Instructions

1. Use a fork to pierce the spaghetti squash holes down the side. Five minutes of a microwave.
2. Preheat the oven to a temperature of 200 ° C.
3. Slice the squash open, lengthwise, with a sharp knife, when the squash is cool enough to touch (5-10 minutes).
4. Cover the seeds with salt and pepper and drizzle the squash with oil.
5. For 40 minutes, roast the squash cut-side down, until quickly pierced by a knife.
6. Mix the soil turkey, onion, parsley, parmesan cheese, salt, and pepper gently in a large bowl. Shape and move meatballs to a greased baking sheet.
7. Bake for 20 minutes in the oven at 400 ° F (200 ° C) until wholly cooked...
8. Take the strings out of the cooled spaghetti squash using a fork and move them to a serving table.
9. Scatter with hot marinara sauce, and chopped parsley scatter.
10. That's right. Enjoy!

**Prep Time** - 10 mins

**Servings** - 4

**Macros** - Calories 196 Fat 12g Carbs 4g Fiber 1g Sugar 2g Protein 17g

# SEAFOOD AND FISH RECIPES

## 80. GREEK SNAPPER ON THE GRILL

### Ingredients

- 12 (8-ounce) snapper or grouper fillets
- ¼ cup olive oil
- One tablespoon Greek seasoning
- 24 (¼-inch-thick) lemon slices
- Tartar sauce

### Instructions

1. Brush the fillets of fish with oil; sprinkle with Greek seasoning uniformly. Cover each fillet with two slices of lemon.
2. Place a large piece of heavy-duty aluminum foil slightly greased over barbecue cooking pan. Place the fish on the foil.
3. Grill fillets, lined with grill top, for 15 minutes over medium-high heat or with a fork until fish flakes. Serve with tartar sauce, whether homemade or purchased from the supermarket.

**Prep Time** - 15 mins

**Servings** - 12

**Macros** - Calories 196 Fat 12g Carbs 4g Fiber 1g Sugar 2g Protein 17g

## 81. SHRIMP AND BLACK BEAN ENCHILADAS

### Ingredient

- 2 (10-ounce) cans red or green of enchilada sauce
- 1 pound of shrimp
- 2 (15-ounce) cans of black beans
- 2 cups Mexican blend shredded cheese
- 12 to 13 small flour tortillas

### Instructions

1. Preheat the oven to 400 degrees Celsius. Add ¼ cup of the sauce (enchiladas) in a skillet. Turn the heat up and add the shrimp. Cook until the shrimp is clean and no longer translucent for about 5 minutes. Remove from the heated bowl.
2. In a 9-by-13-inch baking dish, arrange the enchiladas. Place on a tortilla one peas lunch, three to four shrimps, and a slice of cheese. Fold the edges of the tortilla in the baking dish over the filling and seam-side down. Start and blend with the remaining tortillas. Verse the remaining enchilada sauce after all the enchiladas have been prepared. The remaining cheese should be brushed.
3. Bake in the oven until all the cheese has melted for 15 minutes. Remove from the oven, take 5 minutes to rest, then eat.

**Prep Time** - 10 mins

**Servings** - 4

**Macros** - Calories 196 Fat 12g Carbs 4g Fiber 1g Sugar 2g Protein 17g

## 82. HONEY MUSTARD SALMON

### Ingredients:

- 4 (6-ounce) salmon fillets
- 2 tablespoons honey, two tablespoons whole-grain or Dijon mustard, two tablespoons lemon juice
- One clove minced garlic
- Salt and pepper to taste
- Minced parsley for garnish

### Instructions

1. Preheat oven to Fahrenheit 400 degrees. Coat with cooking spray a glass baking dish. In the prepared baking dish, put the salmon, skin-side down.
2. In a small bowl, whisk the sugar, mustard, lemon, garlic, salt, and pepper together. Use a basting brush to cover with the single sauce filet.
3. Move the dish to the oven and fry for 15 to 20 minutes or quickly with a fork until the fish flakes. If needed, garnish with wedges of parsley and lemon, then serve.

**Prep Time** - 5 mins

**Servings** - 4

**Macros** - Calories 296 Fat 10g Carbs 5g Fiber 2g Sugar 3g Protein 18g

## 83. PARMESAN-CRUSTED TILAPIA

### Ingredients:

- ¾ cup freshly grated Parmesan cheese
- Two teaspoons paprika
- One tablespoon chopped flat-leaf parsley
- 4 (4-ounce) tilapia fillets
- One lemon, cut into wedges

### Instructions

1. Preheat the oven to 400 degrees Celsius. Combine the cheese in a shallow dish with the paprika and parsley and season with salt and pepper. In the cheese mixture, blend the fish with olive oil and dredge. Place on a baking sheet lined with foil and bake for 10 to 12 minutes until the fish is opaque in the thickest part. Serve the lemon wedges with the fish

Makes four servings.

**Macros** - 210 calories; 9.3 g fat; 1.3 g carbohydrates; 28.9 g protein; 54 mg cholesterol; 280 mg sodium.

## 84. STEAMED COD WITH GINGER AND SCALLIONS

### Ingredients

- 4 (6- to 8-ounce) skinless cod fillets
- Three tablespoons rice vinegar
- Two tablespoons soy sauce
- Two tablespoons finely grated, peeled fresh ginger, coarse salt and ground pepper
- Six scallions, green parts cut into 3-inch lengths

### Instructions

2. Combine 3 tablespoons of rice vinegar, 2 tablespoons of soy sauce,

and 2 tablespoons of finely grated fresh peeled ginger in a large skillet.

3. Coat on both sides of four skinless cod fillets with coarse salt and ground pepper; put in skillet with a mixture of vinegar. Cover; cook until the fish is nearly opaque for 6 to 8 minutes.

4. In the meantime, cut into 3-inch lengths green parts of 6 scallions; slice thinly lengthwise. Scatter over fish; fry, covered until all fish is opaque, and just wilted scallions, about 2 minutes longer.

**Prep Time** - 10 mins

**Servings** - 4

**Macros** - Calories 296 Fat 10g Carbs 5g Fiber 2g Sugar 3g Protein 18g

## 85. RIOJA STEAMED MUSSELS WITH CHORIZO

### Ingredients

- 1 pound fresh chorizo, casings removed, crumbled
- One huge Spanish onion, sliced
- Kosher salt and freshly cracked black pepper
- 2 pounds black mussels, cleaned and bearded, one bottle Rioja or other dry red wine
- ½ cup coarsely chopped flat-leaf parsley

### Instruction

1. Place the chorizo in a large, heavy pot over high heat with a lid. Cook for about 10 minutes until the fat is made and the meat has browned. Remove the meat from a plate and

hold it with a slotted spoon. In a pinch of salt and pepper, add the onions to the pot and cook until softened for 6 to 8 minutes. Return the chorizo to the pan and drop it in the molds. Pour the wine over it, cover it, and bring it to a boil. Cook for about 4 to 5 minutes until the musk has opened.

2. Remove the lid and remove any unopened molds. Remove very well in the wine and onions until the molds are covered. Garnish and serve immediately with the parsley.

**Prep Time** - 35 mins

**Servings** - 4

**Macros** - Calories 296 Fat 10g Carbs 5g Fiber 2g Sugar 3g Protein 18g

## 86. GRILLED TUNA OVER ARUGULA WITH LEMON VINAIGRETTE

### Ingredients

- 5 ounces sashimi tuna
- One teaspoon extra-virgin olive oil, one teaspoon fresh lemon juice
- 2 cups baby arugula
- One teaspoon capers
- Kosher salt and fresh pepper.

### Instructions

1. Kosher salt and freshly cracked pepper season the tuna.

2. Place the arugula on a plate with capers. In a pan, mix oil and lemon juice with salt and pepper.

3. Heat your grill well to high heat and wash the grill. When the grill is dry, spray oil grate to avoid sticking, then

put tuna on the rack; cook without moving for one minute. Turn over and prepare for a second-minute; remove from heat and set aside on a tray.

4. On the diagonal slice the tuna and place it on top of the salad. Fill with the lemon dressing and eat right away.

**Prep Time** - 20 mins

**Servings** - 6

**Macros** - Calories 156 Fat 10g Carbs 5g Fiber 2g Sugar 3g Protein 18g

## 87. SALMON NOODLE BOWL RECIPE

### Ingredients

- 1 (9 ounces) package refrigerated fettuccine
- 1 pound skinless, boneless 1-inch thick salmon fillet, cut into eight pieces
- Two tablespoons olive oil
- 6 cups packaged fresh baby spinach, ½ cup bottled roasted red or yellow sweet peppers
- ½ cup garlic-stuffed green olives, coarsely chopped, ½ cup reduced-calorie balsamic vinaigrette salad dressing

### Instructions

1. Cook pasta as instructed by the box.
2. In the meantime, wash the fish with an olive oil teaspoon. Sprinkle with salt and black pepper slightly.
3. Place over medium heat a large skillet. Attach the fish to the hot skillet; cook for 8 to 12 minutes or

until the fish starts to flake when checked with a fork, rotating through the cooking once. Remove the fish from the skillet; keep warm and cover.

4. Add to skillet spinach, roasted peppers, olives, and the remaining one tablespoon of olive oil; cook and stir for 1 to 2 minutes or until spinach is wilted.
5. Pasta drain; add to skillet.
6. Toss to coat — season with salt and pepper to taste.
7. Divide into four shallow bowls the pasta mixture; top with fish.

**Prep Time** - 10 Minutes

**Servings** - 6

**Macros** - Calories 366 Fat 18g Carbs 5g Fiber 2g Sugar 3g Protein 15g

## 88. THINK GREEK GROUPER RECIPE

### Ingredients

- 4 (4 ounces) grouper fillets, 1 (10 ounces) package frozen chopped spinach, thawed and squeezed dry
- Two teaspoons salt-free Greek seasoning
- Cooking spray
- One plum tomato, coarsely chopped
- ¼ cup (1 ounce) crumbled basil- and tomato-flavored feta cheese
- Cooked orzo (optional)

### Instructions

1. Sprinkle on both sides of the filets with seasoning. Coat with a cooking spray a large non-stick skillet and position until warm over medium-

high heat. Remove the fish and cook for 3 minutes; remove from heat the skillet.

2. Turn the fish; top with tomato spinach and cheese. Return to skillet and cook for 3 to 4 minutes or until spinach is warm and fish flakes are easily checked with a fork. Serve over cooked orzo immediately.

**Prep Time:** 10 Minutes

**Servings** - 8

**Macros** - Calories 566 Fat 10g Carbs 6g Fiber 2g Sugar 5g Protein 28g

# 89. ROILED HALIBUT WITH GARLIC-CHIVE SOUR CREAM RECIPE

## Ingredients

- Four halibut fillets (about 5 ounces each)
- One tablespoon Italian seasoning
- ¾ cup light sour cream
- Two tablespoons chopped fresh chives
- ½ teaspoon garlic powder

## Instructions

1. Heat the broiler preheat. Coat with cooking spray on a baking sheet.
2. Top with salt, pepper, and Italian seasoning all over the halibut. Move the halibut to the prepared baking sheet and broil on each side for 3 to 5 minutes until the fork is tender.
3. In the meantime, blend and mix well the sour cream, chives, and garlic powder. Serve the halibut with the top spooned sour cream mixture.

**Prep Time:** 5 Minutes

**Servings** - 10

**Macros** - Calories 97 Fat 6g Carbs 5g Fiber 2g Sugar 3g Protein 5g

# 90. LEMON CRUSTED SALMON WITH THE CITRUS HERB SAUCE RECIPE

## Ingredients

- Four salmon fillets (about 5 ounces each)
- Four teaspoons lemon and herb seasoning
- 1 cup of orange juice
- One tablespoon chopped fresh thyme
- One teaspoon dried oregano

## Instructions

1. Heat the oven to 375 degrees. Coat with cooking spray on a baking sheet.
2. Season with salt, pepper and lemon and herb seasoning on both sides of the salmon. Place the salmon on the prepared baking sheet and bake till the salmon is fork-tender for 12 to 15 minutes.
3. In a shallow saucepan over medium heat, whisk together the orange juice, thyme, and oregano. Serve the salmon over the rim with the spooned orange sauce.

**Prep Time:** 10 Minutes

**Servings** - 8

**Macros** - Calories 156 Fat 10g Carbs 5g Fiber 2g Sugar 3g Protein 18g

# 91. TUNA BURGER SANDWICHES RECIPE

## Ingredients

- 2– 6-ounce cans tuna, packed in water
- Six slices cheddar cheese, 1 cup chopped celery
- Small onion, minced
- ¼ cup mayonnaise
- Six hamburger buns

## INSTRUCTIONS

1. Ingredients of the coating on the buns.
2. Wrap in foil made of aluminum.
3. Place at 350°F for 15 minutes in the oven. Serve hot.

**Prep Time**: 10 Minutes

**Servings** - 4

**Macros** - Calories 186 Fat 10g Carbs 5g Fiber 2g Sugar 3g Protein 12g

# 92. BAKED FISH RECIPE

## Ingredients

- 2 pounds white fish, your choice
- 10¾ ounce can cream of mushroom soup
- 1¼ cups sour cream, or plain yogurt
- ½ cup buttered crumbs, or cracker crumbs
- One tablespoon poppy seeds

## INSTRUCTIONS

1. Put the fish in a greased casserole dish of 2 thirds.
2. Layer soup and sour cream in a small bowl. Sprinkle over fish.

3. Attach seeds of poppy to the crumbs. Sprinkle with the edge.
4. Bake for 30 minutes at 425 ° F or until fish flakes easily.

**Prep Time:** 15 Minutes

**Servings** - 8

**Macros** - Calories 147 Fat 5g Carbs 5g Fiber 2g Sugar 3g Protein 8g

# 93. BAKED MOZZARELLA FISH RECIPE

## Ingredients

- 2 pounds thick flounder, or sole, fillets
- Salt and pepper to taste
- ½ teaspoon dried oregano
- 1 cup shredded mozzarella cheese
- One large fresh tomato, thinly sliced

## Instructions

1. Big baking dish of butter. Arrange a single layer of trout. Add salt, pepper, and oregano to sprinkle.
2. Top with slices of sliced cheese and tomato.
3. Bake, cover, 10 to 15 minutes at 425 ° F, or quickly until fish flakes.

**Prep Time:** 10 Minutes

**Servings**- 6 to 8

**Macros** - Calories 156 Fat 6g Carbs 5g Fiber 2g Sugar 3g Protein 8g

# 94. SHRIMP AND FETA SCAMPI RECIPE

## Ingredients

- 1 (8 ounces) package spaghetti

- 1½ pounds peeled and deveined Shrimp
- 1 (10 ounces) package frozen snow peas or fresh sugar snap peas
- Four green onions, sliced
- ⅓ cup reduced-fat olive oil vinaigrette, ¼ teaspoon freshly ground black pepper, ½ cup crumbled reduced-fat feta cheese

## Instructions

1. Put 2 quarters of water in a large casserole to boil. Remove pasta and cook 9 minutes, uncovered.
2. Add shrimp; cook for 3 minutes, uncovered, or until shrimp turn pink.
3. The pea pods should be put in a colander. Drain the pea pods with the pasta and shrimp.
4. Switch the mixture to a large bowl.
5. Add onions, dressing, and pepper; toss gently. Sprinkle with feta cheese that is crumbled.

**Prep Time**: 5 Minutes

**Servings** - 10

**Macros** - Calories 218 Fat 10g Carbs 5g Fiber 2g Sugar 3g Protein 12g

## 95. STEAMED MUSSELS IN WHITE WINE

## Ingredients

- 4 pounds fresh mussels
- 1/2 cup of white wine, 1/4 cup of shallots (chopped)
- Two cloves of garlic (thinly sliced, not cut or minced)
- Freshly ground black pepper (to taste)

- Four tablespoons butter (1/2 stick), two tablespoons parsley (chopped)
- Fresh lemon juice (to taste)

## Instructions

1. The ingredients were obtained.
2. Pick the muscles, wash them, and de-beard them. Rinse with cold water.
3. Add the wine, garlic, shallots, and black pepper in a large stockpot or soup pot and bring to a boil over high heat.
4. Attach the mussels and cover the pan with a tightly fitted lid. Reduce to medium-high heat and cook for 5 to 6 minutes or until most molds have been removed. Don't overcook or rubbery may become the molds.
5. Remove butter and parsley and whisk until the butter has melted in the milk.
6. Complete with a fresh lemon juice squeeze.
7. Serve for soaking up the fragrant sauce in large bowls with the cooking liquid, along with plenty of crusty bread. There will also be a different box for the empty shells in handy.

**Prep Time** - 30 mins

**Servings** - 8

**Macros** - 966 Calories, 32g Fat, 48g Carbs, 111g Protein

## 96. FRESH AND FLAVORFUL TOMATO SALSA

## Ingredients

- Four medium tomatoes

- Two cloves garlic (mashed and finely minced), Three tablespoons finely chopped onions
- 1 to 2 tablespoons jalapeno pepper (minced)
- Two heaping tablespoons cilantro (finely chopped), Two tablespoons fresh lime juice
- Freshly ground black pepper (to taste)

## Instructions

1. The ingredients were obtained.
2. The tomatoes are the heart. Remove the seeds and roughly chop them.
3. Combine the chopped tomatoes, garlic, onion, chili pepper, coriander, and lime juice in a pan. Mix the ingredients together.
4. Attach salt, and black pepper freshly ground to taste.
5. Cover and cool before serving time

**Prep Time** - 20 min

**Servings** - 6

**Macros** - Calories 45kcal Fat 0gCarbs 10g Protein 2g

## 97. TUNA ALFREDO CASSEROLE

## Ingredients

- 3 cups Mafalda (mini lasagna), mostaccioli noodles, or penne pasta
- 1/2 cup basil pesto
- One 10-ounce container refrigerated cheese or plain Alfredo sauce
- One 12-ounce tuna (drained and chunked)
- 1/3 cup Parmesan cheese (grated)

## Instructions

1. Oven preheats to 400 F. Brings to a boil a big pot of water.
2. Cook the pasta as instructed, taking one minute off the time of cooking. Drain well when the pasta is almost al dente.
3. Alternatively, in a medium bowl, add pesto and Alfredo sauce and blend together. Remove the pasta and tuna cooked, then gently combine.
4. Pour the tuna mixture into a2-quarter grated glass baking dish and top with Parmesan cheese.
5. Bake it for 15 to 20 minutes until the cheese is melted and the casserole is moist.

**Prep Time** - 15 min

**Servings** - 6

**Macros** - Calories 64kcal Fat 0gCarbs 10g Protein 4g

## 98. CRAB AND SHRIMP SEAFOOD BISQUE

## Ingredients

- Three tablespoons butter, Two tablespoons green onion (chopped), Two tablespoons celery (chopped), Three tablespoons all-purpose flour
- 2 ½ cups of milk, 1/2 teaspoon of ground black pepper
- One tablespoon tomato paste, two tablespoon sherry wine
- 1 cup heavy whipping cream
- 8 ounces of crab meat, 8 ounces cooked shrimp (or other seafood)

## Instructions

1. The ingredients were obtained.

2. Melt the butter over medium-low heat in a Dutch oven or large saucepan; add the chopped onion and celery. Stir, sauté, until tender.
3. Stir the flour until well mixed into the butter and vegetables. Continue to cook for about 2 minutes, stirring.
4. Heat the milk over medium heat in another saucepan.
5. Slowly pour in the heated milk and cook and mix until thickened.
6. Remove the black pepper, tomato paste, and heavy cream that is freshly ground.
7. Puree the soup at this level, if desired, in a blender or food processor (see tips), and then return it to the saucepan.
8. Remove the lobster, the shrimp, the sherry. Bring it to low heat.
9. Serve warm.

**Prep Time** - 15 mins

**Servings** - 4

**Macros** - 421Calories, 20gFat, 29gCarbs, 30gProtein

## 99. SHRIMP FRIED RICE

### Ingredients

- 4 ounces shrimp (frozen, uncooked, unshelled)
- 4 ounces ham (cooked)
- One medium onion, two green onions
- Two eggs
- 1/2 cup of peas, 4 cups rice, 4 to 5 tablespoons oil (for stir-frying, or as needed)

**Marinade:**

- One tablespoon oyster sauce (or to taste)
- One tablespoon soy sauce (or to taste)
- One teaspoon salt (or to taste)
- pepper to taste
- One teaspoon cornstarch (mixed with 1 1/2 teaspoons water)

### Instructions

1. Under hot running water, run the frozen shrimp and pat dry with paper towels.
2. Devein and shell.
3. Cut into tiny pieces.
4. Attach the ingredients of the marinade and marinate 15 minutes.
5. Dice the tomato, ham, and green onion.
6. Smoothly beat the eggs with chopsticks, apply a salt brush, and mix.* Remove.
7. Heat the wok, then add a spoonful of oil.
8. Pour 1/2 of the egg mixture into the wok once the oil is ready and cook over medium heat.
9. Cook the other half like that.
10. Cut the egg into thin strips for later saving.
11. Attach two cubicles of oil or whenever needed.
12. Stir-fry the onion and shrimp for a few moments on high heat when the oil is hot.
13. Do the same for the green peas and then for the diced ham.
14. Attach 1 to 2 cubic meters of oil, turn the heat to high, and stir-fry the rice.
15. If needed, add a little soy and oyster sauce.

16. Remove the other ingredients and mix thoroughly (except the egg and green onion).
17. Serve the fried rice on top with the egg strips and garnish with the green onion.

**Prep Time** - 15 mins

**Servings** - 4

**Macros** - 852 Calories, 7g Fat, 162g Carbs, 30g Protein

## 100. EASY BACON-WRAPPED SCALLOPS

### Ingredients

- 24 large sea scallops (about 2 pounds)
- 12 slices bacon (partially cooked)
- Dash seasoned pepper

### Instructions

1. The ingredients were obtained.
2. Cook the bacon gently until cooked in part, but not crisp and flexible.
3. Under running cold water, clean scallops, pat dry with paper towels. This is an active muscle and should be removed if you find any tag-like bits on the surface of the scallops. Just pinch it to clear it with your fingertips.
4. Cut each slice of bacon in half crosswise; wrap around a scallop every half and secure it with a toothpick.
5. Sprinkle with seasoned pepper scallops thinly— Preheat broiler.
6. In a broiling pan, put scallops on a rack.

7. Broil from heat for 8 to 10 minutes for 4 to 5 inches, or until all sides of the scallops are opaque, occasionally using tongs to turn scallops so that the bacon browns evenly.
8. Serve as an entrance or an appetizer.

**Prep Time** - 15 mins

**Servings** - 24

**Macros** – 29 Calories 0g Fat 1g Carbs 5g Protein

## 101. SHRIMP AND RICE SALAD WITH PEAS AND CELERY

### Ingredients

- 1 1/2 cup cooked rice
- 1 pound shrimp, 1/2 cup diced celery
- Three green onions, thinly sliced, Two tablespoons finely chopped red bell pepper
- 1 cup fresh or frozen green peas, cooked until just tender
- 1/1/4 teaspoon black of pepper, 1/2 teaspoon of celery seed, 1/2 to 3/4 cup mayonnaise, Two tablespoons dill pickle juice, 2 teaspoons of salt

### Instructions

1. Cook the rice as instructed by the box. Remove from heat and totally relaxed.
2. Peel the crevices. Make a shallow cut with a thin, sharp knife to the back of a shrimp. Cut the dark vein; thoroughly rinse. Repeat with the rest of the shrimp.
3. Take a casserole of water to a boil; add the shrimp, and reduce the heat

to medium. Simmer the shrimps for 3 minutes until it turns pink and opaque. The time depends on the shrimp's size. Let them cool down the shrimp and chop them roughly.

4. Combine the seafood, celery, onions, beans, and red pepper bell in a serving bowl. Sprinkle with seeds of salt, pepper, and celery.

5. Apply the cooled rice to the mixture of shrimps; apply the pickle juice mayonnaise and dill and blend gently.

6. Taste the seasonings and change them.

**Prep Time** - 20 mins

**Servings** - 4

**Macros** - 658 Calories 28g Fat 66g Carbs 34g Protein

# VEGETARIAN RECIPES

## 102. SLOW COOKER CHICKPEA SWEET POTATO STEW

### Ingredients

- One medium yellow onion, chopped
- 2 15 oz cans garbanzo beans, drained
- 1 pound sweet potatoes, peeled and chopped
- One tablespoon garlic, minced, 1/2 teaspoon Kosher salt, 1/4 teaspoon coarse ground black pepper, one teaspoon ground ginger, 1 1/2 teaspoons ground cumin, one teaspoon ground coriander, 1/4 teaspoon ground cinnamon
- 4 cups vegetable broth, fat-free, 4 cups fresh baby spinach

### Instructions

1. Except for the spinach, add the ingredients together and cook for 8 minutes at high pressure.
2. Quick-release, pour in the spinach and cover it for 2 minutes until it is wilted.
3. (You can also sweat the garlic and onions first, but if you do, add a teaspoon of olive oil.)

**Prep Time** - 15 mins

**Servings** - 6

**Macros** - Calories: 165kcal, Carbohydrates: 32.3g, Protein: 6.3g, Fat: 2.2g, Saturated Fat: 1.4g, Sodium: 751mg, Fiber: 6.2g, Sugar: 5.4g

## 103. CHICKPEA TOMATO SOUP WITH ROSEMARY

### Ingredient

- 1 tsp olive of oil, 1/2 cup chopped onion.
- 1/2 cup of diced carrot, 1/2 cup of diced celery, two garlic cloves, minced
- 15 oz cans chickpeas, rinsed and drained, 28 oz can crushed tomatoes
- 3 cups reduced-sodium chicken broth, or vegetable broth for vegetarians, one fresh rosemary sprig, two-bay of leaves
- 2 tbsp of chopped fresh basil, fresh black pepper, 2 cups fresh baby spinach, 1/4 cup shredded parmesan cheese, plus extra optional for garnish

### Instructions

1. Heat oil in a large non-stick skillet. Add carrots, celery, onion, garlic, and saute for around 6 to 8 minutes until tender and fragrant. Add the broth, onions, chickpeas, parmesan cheese, and pepper to the crockpot. Add the rosemary, basil, and bay leaves, cover, and cook for 6 hours at low.
2. Upon completion, add the spinach. Cut bay leaves, rosemary sprig, and season to taste. Ladle soup in bowls and, if desired, top with extra parmesan cheese.

**Prep Time** -10 mins

**Servings** - 4

**Macros:** 11/2 cups, Calories: 215kcal, Carbohydrates: 36g, Protein: 9g, Fat: 3g, Fiber: 6g, Sugar: 6g

## 104. VEGAN AFRICAN PEANUT STEW

### Ingredients

- 15 oz can of chickpeas (drained & rinsed)
- 4 cups vegetable stock
- 1/2 teaspoon salt, One teaspoon cumin, 1/2 teaspoon ground coriander, 1/4 teaspoon cayenne, 15 oz can of diced tomatoes (including juices)
- 4-5 cups sweet potatoes (cut into 2-inch cubes; roughly two medium sweet potatoes), 1/2 cup all-natural peanut butter (creamy or crunchy)
- One onion (diced), Four cloves garlic (minced), 1-inch ginger (finely grated)
- Just before serving
- Four handfuls spinach (chopped)

### Instructions

1. In a 6-quarter slow cooker, combine all ingredients and cook at low for 6-8 hours.
2. Remove and cook the spinach for 15 minutes.
3. Mash the sweet potato until thickening of the stew. Enjoy!
4. In a large freezer bag, combine all ingredients without stock and spinach. Squeeze as much air as you can and freeze flat. Freeze for up to three months.

5. Thaw thoroughly and cook according to the above directions.

**Prep Time** - 15 mins

**Servings** - 8

**Macros** - Serving: 1/8 of batch | Calories: 263kcal | Carbohydrates: 36g | Protein: 10g | Fat: 9g | Saturated Fat: 1g | Fiber: 7g | Sugar: 9g |

## 105. SLOW COOKER WHITE BEAN STEW

### Ingredients

- 2 (15 ounce) cans navy beans
- One large carrot, peeled and diced small
- 1/4 cup celery, diced small, 1/2 cup yellow onion, diced small, Three cloves garlic, minced
- 1/2 teaspoon crushed red pepper, One teaspoon dried rosemary, One teaspoon dried thyme, One teaspoon dried oregano
- 2 1/2 cups low sodium vegetable broth, 1 (14 ounces) can diced tomatoes, 3 cups kale, chopped, 1/2 cup low-fat parmesan cheese, shredded

### Instructions

1. Drain and rinse the navy beans.
2. Add all ingredients in a slow cooker, excluding kale and parmesan. Cover and cook for 4 hours on low or 2 hours on high add the kale and cover and cook for an additional 30 minutes on high or until wilted. Ladle into serving bowls and top with parmesan. Serve and enjoy!

**Prep Time** - 10 mins

**Servings** - 6

**Macros** - Yields: | Serving Size: 1 1/2 cups | Calories: 238 | Total Fat: 4g | Saturated Fat: 2g |Carbohydrates: 37g | Fiber: 10g | Sugar: 4g | Protein: 16g |

## 106. SLOW COOKER WILD RICE AND MUSHROOM SOUP

### Ingredients

- 1 large onion, halved then thinly sliced, four cloves of garlic, minced
- 700 g of mushrooms
- 150 ml dry white wine, 400 ml of hot vegetable stock
- 180 g white and wild rice mix, 3 tbsp cream
- Small bunch fresh parsley, chopped, Salt, Black pepper

### Instructions

1. Add the onion, garlic, and sliced mushrooms to the slow cooker and pour over the white wine. Cook for 2 1/2 hours, stirring and scraping down the sides after the first hour if you can.
2. When the vegetables are very soft, add the vegetable stock and rice and mix well. Cook on high for a further 2 hours, or until the rice is fully cooked.
3. Add the cream and fresh parsley, and season to taste. Serve immediately.

**Prep Time** - 10 mins

**Servings** - 3

**Macros**        - Calories:        345kcal, Carbohydrates: 61.5g, Protein: 17.1g, Fat: 3.2g, Saturated Fat: 1.6g, Fiber: 6.2g, Sugar: 9.2g

## 107. SLOW COOKER RATATOUILLE

### Ingredients

- 2 Tablespoons coconut oil (or ghee)
- One large onion, chopped, six cloves garlic, minced, one large eggplant, chopped, one orange bell pepper, chopped, four summer squash/zucchini squash
- 1 cup chopped grape tomatoes, 1 cup fresh basil, chopped
- 2 Tablespoons tomato paste, one teaspoon dried oregano, teaspoon ground pepper, 1/2–1 teaspoon sea salt, 1/4 teaspoon crushed red pepper (optional)

### Instructions

1. In a large slow-cooker, cover and cook all ingredients except basil. Cook at high for 3-4 hours or at low for 5-6 hours). When the vegetables have softened, the ratatouille is ready, but they are not mushy. If you're concerned that the ratatouille is too watery, remove the last hour's slow cooker lid and cook up. Stir gently in fresh basil just before serving. Serve as the main entry warm or cold as a side or over a whole grain like quinoa or rice.

**Prep Time** - 20 mins

**Servings** - 8

**Macros**- Calories: 127 Sugar: 9g Fat: 5g C arbohydrates: 23g Fiber: 10g Protein: 5g

# 108. SLOW COOKER COCONUT CURRIED EGGPLANT

## Ingredients

- 4 cups chopped eggplant (peeled, if desired)
- 4 cups chopped zucchini, 6 oz can of tomato paste
- One medium yellow onion, four cloves garlic, minced, one tablespoon curry powder, one tablespoon garam masala, 1/4 teaspoon cayenne pepper, 1/4 teaspoon cumin, one teaspoon salt
- 15 oz can of coconut milk, 1/4 cup vegetable broth (optional)
- chopped fresh parsley or cilantro for garnish

## Instructions

2. Place garlic and onion in a chopper to finely chop.
3. Add chopped onion and garlic mixture, eggplant, zucchini, spices, tomato paste, and coconut milk to your slow cooker. Stir everything together. At this point, if the combination seems too thick, you can add in a little vegetable broth. Cook on low for 4-5 hours. Garnish with fresh parsley or cilantro. Serve warm with rice and naan.

**Prep time** - 15 mins

**Servings** - 4

**Macros** - Calories: 321Sugar: 16gFat: 24g

Carbohydrates: 27gFiber: 5gProtein: 6g

# 109. VEGETARIAN TORTILLA LASAGNA

## Ingredients

- One can of diced tomatoes with basil, oregano, and garlic
- 1 cup chunky salsa, One can (6 ounces) tomato paste, 1/2 teaspoon ground cumin
- Two cans (15-1/2 ounces each) hominy, rinsed and drained
- One can (15 ounces) no-salt-added black beans, rinsed and drained, Three flour tortillas, 2 cups of shredded Monterey Jack cheese.
- 1/4 cup sliced ripe olives

## Instructions

1. Split 3 25x3-in. Heavy-duty foil strips; crisscross, so they appear like wheel spokes. Place pieces in a round 5-qt on the bottom and up the sides. Slow to cook. Coat strips with spray for cooking.
2. Combine tomatoes, sauce, tomato paste, and cumin in a large bowl. Incorporate hominy and beans. Put a tortilla on the slow cooker's rim. Top with a third of the cheese and hominy mixture. Repeat twice the layers. Sprinkle with olives— cover and cook for 3-1/2 hours at low or until warm.
3. Transfer the lasagna to a platter using film strips as handles. Let stand before cutting into wedges for 5 minutes.

**Prep Time** - 20

**Servings** - 8

Macros - One slice: 335 calories, 12g fat (6g saturated fat), 41g carbohydrate (6g sugars, 8g fiber), 15g protein.

## 110. VEGETARIAN BUFFALO DIP

### Ingredients

- 1 cup sour cream
- 8 ounces cream cheese, softened, one envelope ranch salad dressing mix
- 2 cups shredded sharp cheddar cheese;
- one can (15 ounces) black beans, rinsed and drained
- 8 ounces fresh mushrooms, chopped, 1 cup Buffalo wing sauce
- Optional: Sliced green onions and tortilla chips

### Instructions

1. Combine sour cream, cream cheese, and ranch dressing mix in a bowl until smooth. Stir in the next four ingredients. Transfer to a 3- or 4-qt. Slow cooker. Cook, covered, on high for 1-1/2 hours. If desired, sprinkle with green onion and serve with tortilla chips

**Prep Time** - 10 mins

**Servings** - 6

**Macros** - 1/4 cup: 113 calories, 8g fat (5g saturated fat), 21mg cholesterol, 526mg sodium, 5g carbohydrate (1g sugars, 1g fiber), 4g protein.

## 111. SPICED ACORN SQUASH

### Ingredients

- 3/4 cup packed brown sugar
- One teaspoon ground cinnamon
- One teaspoon ground nutmeg
- Two small acorn squash, halved and seeded
- 3/4 cup raisins
- Four tablespoons butter
- 1/2 cup water

### Instructions

1. In a small bowl, add brown sugar, cinnamon, and nutmeg; spoon into half of the squash. Sprinkle with the grapes. Top each butter with one cubic cubicle. Of heavy-duty foil, cover each half individually, securing securely.
2. In a 5-qt— slow cooker, add water. Place squash in the cut side upside of the slow cooker (packets can be stacked). Cook on high 3-1/2 to 4 hours, sealed, or until tender squash. Carefully open the foil so that steam can escape.

**Prep Time** - 15 mins

**Servings** - 4

**Macros** - Per squash half: 433 calories, 12g fat (7g saturated fat), 31mg cholesterol, 142mg sodium, 86g carbohydrate (63g sugars, 5g fiber), 3g protein.

## 112. SLOW-COOKER POTLUCK BEANS

### Ingredients

- 1 cup brewed coffee

- 1/2 cup packed brown sugar
- 1/4 cup spicy brown mustard
- Two tablespoons molasses
- Two cans (16 ounces each) butter beans, Two cans (16 ounces each) kidney beans, Two cans (16 ounces each) navy beans

## Instructions

1. In a greased 3- or 4-qt. Slow cooker, mix the first four ingredients. Rinse and drain beans; stir into coffee mixture. Cook, sealed, 4-5 hours on low until the flavors are combined.
2. Freeze option: Freeze cooled beans in freezer containers. To use, partially thaw in refrigerator overnight. Heat through in a covered saucepan, stirring gently and adding a little water if necessary.

**Prep Time** - 10 mins

**Servings** - 12

**Macros** - 1/2 cup: 243 calories, 0 fat (0 saturated fat), 0 cholesterol, 538mg sodium, 50g carbohydrate (13g sugars, 10g fiber), 14g protein.

# 113. SLOW-COOKER BAKED POTATOES

## Ingredients

- Six medium russet potatoes
- Three tablespoons butter softened, Sour cream, butter, crumbled bacon, minced chives
- Three garlic cloves, minced
- 1 cup of water
- Salt and pepper to taste

- Guacamole, shredded cheddar cheese, minced fresh cilantro, optional

## Instructions

1. Pierce potatoes with a fork several times. Mix the butter and garlic in a small bowl. Rub potatoes with butter mixture. Wrap each tightly with a piece of foil.
2. Pour water into a 6-qt. Slow cooker; add potatoes. Cook, covered, on low 8-10 hours or until tender. Season and top as desired.

**Prep Time** - 10 mins

**Servings** - 6

**Macros** - 1 potato: 217 calories, 6g fat (4g saturated fat), 15mg cholesterol, 59mg sodium, 38g carbohydrate (2g sugars, 5g fiber), 5g protein.

# 114. SLOW COOKER TACO BAKE

## Ingredients

- One package Mission® Gluten Free Soft Taco Tortillas (6 counts)
- 1 pound lean ground chicken or turkey
- 1 28 ounces can red enchilada sauce
- 1 cup shredded cheese of choice, divided
- 1 4 ounces can slice of black olives, divided

## Instruction

1. Brown ground turkey in a medium to high heat skillet. Cut a tortilla into strips and apply to the browned meat the tortilla strips together with

the enchilada sauce, 1/2 cup cheese, and 1/2 olives. Shake to mix.

2. In a slow cooker, add the mixture. Cover with a few more tortillas, the remaining cheese, and olives on the cover — cover and cook for 4 hours on medium, or for 8 hours on low.

3. Enjoy slices of Greek yogurt, light sour cream, guacamole, or avocado if you wish.

**Prep time** - 5 min

**Servings** - 1

**Macros**- Calories 231, Fat 8g, Carbohydrates 20g, Fiber 4g, Sugar 3g, Protein 20g

## 115. WHITE BEANS AND SAUSAGE IN THE CROCKPOT

### Ingredient

- 4 cups white beans
- 1 (25-ounce) jar crushed tomatoes
- One tablespoon garlic powder
- One tablespoon Celtic sea salt
- 12 ounces kielbasa sausage

### Instruction

1. In a big pan, put navy beans and cover with water. Leave overnight at room temperature. Drain the beans and pour into a crockpot's bowl the next day. Cover with water the seeds and stir in the onions, garlic powder, salt, and sausage.

2. Place on the lid, place on the crockpot, and cook for 8 hours or until the beans are tender. Apply to taste more salt or garlic powder. Serve.

**Prep time** - 10 min

**Serves** 8

**Macros** - Calories 2310.92 cal FAT 66.98g CARBS310.36 g PROTEIN 150.54

# DESSERT RECIPES

## 116. SLOW COOKER PEANUT BUTTER CHOCOLATE CAKE

### Ingredients

- 15.25 oz. devil's food cake mix
- 1 cup of water
- 1/2 cup salted butter, melted
- Three eggs
- 8 oz. pkg. mini Reese's peanut butter cups
- For the topping
- 1 cup creamy peanut butter
- 3 Tbsp. powdered sugar
- Ten bite-size Reese's peanut butter cups

### Instructions

1. Mix the cake mixture, ice, butter, and eggs in a large bowl until smooth. Some lumps are all right, that's all right. Cut the cups of the mini peanut butter.
2. Cleaner nonstick spray on the slow cooker. Add the butter to the cooker slowly and spread over an even layer.
3. Cover and cook on HIGH during the cooking time for 2 hours without opening the lid.
4. Remove the cake from the heat when the cooking time is finished to keep it from continuing to cook.
5. Place the peanut butter in a small pan placed on the stovetop over medium heat. Stir until melted and smooth, observe as it burns hard. To smooth, add the powdered sugar and whisk.
6. Pour over the butter of the sweetened peanut

**Preparation Time** - 15 min

**Servings** - 10

**Macros** - Calories: 607kcal | Carbohydrates: 57g | Protein: 13g | Fat: 39g | Saturated Fat: 13g

## 117. CROCKPOT APPLE PUDDING CAKE

### Ingredients

- 2 cups all-purpose flour, 2/3 cup plus 1/4 cup sugar divided
- Three teaspoons baking powder, One teaspoon salt
- 1/2 cup butter cold, 1 cup milk, Four apples I used Gala Apples, peeled and diced
- 1 1/2 cups orange juice, 1/2 cup honey or light brown sugar
- 2 Tablespoons butter melted, 1 Teaspoon cinnamon

### Instructions

1. Mix the flour, 2/3 cup sugar, baking powder, and salt. Cut the butter until you have coarse crumbs in the mixture.
2. Remove the milk from the crumbs until moistened.
3. Grease a 4 or 5 qt crockpot's bottom and sides. Spoon the batter into the crockpot's bottom and spread evenly. Place the diced apples evenly over the mixture.

4. Whisk together the orange juice, honey, butter, remaining sugar and cinnamon in a medium-sized pan. Garnish the apples.

5. Place the crockpot opening with a clean kitchen towel, place the lid on. It prevents condensation from reaching the crockpot from the cover. Place the crockpot on top and cook until apples are tender for 2 to 3 hours.

6. Serve hot.

**Preparation Time** - 20 min

**Servings** - 10

**Macros** - Calories 405 Fat 9g Saturated Fat 3g Carbohydrates 79g Fiber 2g Sugar 63g Protein 3g

## 118. CROCKPOT BROWNIE COOKIES

### Ingredients

- One box brownie mix
- Two eggs
- 1/4 c butter melted, 1/2 c mini chocolate chips
- 1/2 c chopped walnuts optional
- Eight slices cookie dough slices or heaping tbsp out of a tub

### Instructions

1. If desired, combine your brownie mixture with butter, eggs, chocolate chips, and nuts.

2. Sprinkle with non-stick spray the inside of your crockpot.

3. Place eight slices of ready-made cookie dough or pile tbsp of it on the bottom.

4. In your slow cooker, pour brownie mixture on top and smooth out evenly.

5. Put on the lid and cook on top for 2 hours.

6. To get both textures in your meal, scoop from the middle out to the edge for each serving. If desired, serve warm for best results, top with ice cream.

**Prep time** - 15 min

Servings - 10

**Macros** -Calories 452, Fat 21g, Saturated Fat 7g, Carbohydrates 59g, Sugar 38g, Protein 5g

## 119. CROCKPOT CHOCOLATE CARAMEL MONKEY BREAD

### Ingredients

- 1/2 tbsp sugar, 1/4 tsp ground cinnamon
- 15 oz buttermilk biscuits 2 7.5 oz cans
- 20 milk chocolate-covered caramels such as ROLO or Hershey's Kisses unwrapped
- caramel sauce for topping (optional)
- chocolate sauce for topping (optional)

### Instructions

1. Mix sugar and cinnamon and set aside.

2. Fill a parchment paper crockpot, cover up to the bottom.

3. Wrap 1 buttermilk biscuit dough around one chocolate candy to cover the candy completely, pinching the seam closed. Place the biscuit-

wrapped candy in the crockpot bottom, start in the middle of the crockpot and work your way to the sides. Continue to wrap candy and put it in the crockpot, leaving roughly 1/2 inch between each. Repeat these steps with sweets wrapped in the second layer of biscuit. Sprinkle the remaining cinnamon-sugar mixture on top when using all the dough and confectionery.

4. Cover the crockpot and cook for 1 1/2 hours on the lower side. Once cooked, remove the lid and let cool slightly. Use the edges of the parchment paper to lift the monkey bread out of the crockpot and transfer it to a wire cooling rack. Allow cooling for at least 10-15 minutes.

5. Cut off any excess parchment paper around the edge when ready to serve. In a shallow bread or bowl, put monkey bread and drizzle with chocolate and caramel sauces. Caution: Monkey bread can still be hot in the middle. Second, draw from the insiders for the best results.

**Prep TIme** - 10 min

**Servings** - 6

**Macros** - 337kcal | Fat: 16g | Saturated Fat: 4g | Carbohydrates: 44g | Fiber: 1g | Sugar: 12g | Protein: 5g |

# 120. SLOW COOKER COFFEE CAKE

**Ingredient**

- 2 1/2 cups of all-purpose flour, 1 1/2 cups of brown sugar packed
- 2/3 cup vegetable oil, 1 1/3 cups almond milk or cow's milk
- Two teaspoons baking powder, 1/2 teaspoon baking soda, One teaspoon ground cinnamon, One teaspoon white vinegar, One teaspoon salt
- Two eggs
- 1/2 cup chopped nuts optional

**Instructions**

1. In a large bowl, whisk in flour, brown sugar, and salt. Remove the oil until it is crumbly mixed.

2. In the flour mixture, combine the baking powder, baking soda, and cinnamon with a wooden spoon or spatula. In a measuring cup, place milk, oil, eggs, and vinegar and whisk until the eggs are pounded, then add to the flour mixture and stir until mixed (batter may be slightly lumpy).

3. Spray a nonstick cooking spray 5-7Qt slow cooker or line with a slow cooker liner (sprayed with spray cooking). Pour into the crockpot with the batter.

4. Sprinkle the cake batter's nuts over the end.

5. Place a large paper towel on top of the crockpot insert and place the lid on top of it. Cook on high for 1 1/2 to 2 1/2 hours or until a toothpick is used to clean the edges. The center may be a bit underdone on top.

6. Serve warm directly from the crockpot or store for up to 3 days in an airtight container. Use the slow cooker liner to serve efficiently. You

can pick up the entire box, peel it off, and help the cake that way.

7. Use a 9x13 "pan sprayed with non-stick cooking spray to bake in a conventional oven and bake at 350 ° for about 35-45 minutes.

**Prep Time** - 10 min

**Servings** - 10 to 12

**Macros** | Calories: 411kcal | Carbohydrates: 56g | Protein: 6g | Fat: 19g | Saturated Fat: 3g | Fiber: 2g | Sugar: 33g

## 121. SLOW COOKER APPLE PEAR CRISP

### Ingredients

- Four apples, peeled and cut into 1/2-inch slices
- 3 Bosc pears, peeled and cut into 1/2-inch slices
- 1/3 cup light brown sugar
- One tablespoon all-purpose flour, One tablespoon lemon juice, 1/2 teaspoon ground cinnamon, 1/4 teaspoon kosher salt
- Pinch of ground nutmeg

### FOR THE TOPPING

- 3/4 cup all-purpose flour
- 3/4 cup old fashioned oats
- 1/2 cup chopped pecans
- 1/3 cup light brown sugar
- 1/2 teaspoon ground cinnamon
- 1/2 teaspoon kosher salt
- Eight tablespoons unsalted butter, cut into cubes

### Instructions

1. Combine flour, oats, pecans, sugar, cinnamon, and salt to make the topping. Use your hands to press the butter into the dry ingredients until it looks like coarse crumbs; set aside.
2. Coat lightly with a non-stick spray on the inside of a 4-qt slow cooker: put apples, pears in the slow cooker. Add brown sugar, flour, juice of lemon, cinnamon, salt, and nutmeg. Sprinkle with reserved topping, gently pressing the crumbs into the butter using your fingertips.
3. Layer the slow cooker with a clean dishtowel. Cover and cook for 2-3 hours at low heat or for 90 minutes at high temperature, remove the dishtowel and continue to cook, uncovered until the top is browned and apples are tender for about 1 hour.
4. Serve cold.

**Prep Time** - 15 min

**Servings** - 8

**Macros** - Calories: 267kcal | Carbohydrates: 27g | Protein: 3g | Fat: 17g | Saturated Fat: 7g | Fiber: 4g | Sugar: 16g.

## 122. PERFECT SLOW COOKER CHEESECAKE

### Ingredients

### For the Crust:

- 1 1/2 cups graham cracker crumbs, about 12 whole crackers
- Six tablespoons melted butter

### For the Cheesecake Filling:

- 24 ounces cream cheese
- 1 1/2 cups sour cream, 1 1/4 cups granulated sugar
- Five large eggs
- Three tablespoons all-purpose flour
- One tablespoon vanilla extract
- 1/2 teaspoon salt

## Instructions

1. Switch on the low a6-quarter slow oval cooker. At the bottom of the crock, lay a large piece of parchment paper and cover with nonstick cooking spray. In the food processor, put the graham crackers and pulse them into crumbs. Then pour in the milk, then pump to mix again. Pour the crumbs into the crock and press the bottom uniformly.
2. Remove the bowl of the food processor and add the cream cheese and sugar. Up to smooth pulse. Scrape, add sour cream, eggs, flour, vanilla, and salt. Puree until very smooth.
3. Pour over the crust the filling. Cover the crock and cook slowly for 5-7 hours until clean comes out a skewer inserted in the center. Wipe the moisture off the lid, so on top of the cheesecake, it does not drip down.
4. For at least 3 hours, move the crock to the refrigerator and chill. Carefully bring the whole cheesecake through the edges of the paper out of the bowl. Peel, cut, and serve the paperback!

**Prep Time** - 10 min

**Serving** - 20

**Macros** - Calories: 278kcal, carbohydrates: 20g, Protein: 4g, Fat: 20g, saturated fat: 11g, sugar: 15g

## 123. SLOW COOKER LEMON CAKE

### Ingredients

- 1 3/4 cups of all-purpose flour, 1/2 cup yellow cornmeal
- 3/4 cup butter, softened, 1 1/4 cups sugar, 1 cup sour cream, 1 cup confectioners' sugar
- Two eggs
- One tablespoon grated lemon zest, one teaspoon vanilla extract, 1 1/2 teaspoons poppy seeds, 2 1/2 tablespoons lemon juice, One teaspoon baking powder, One teaspoon baking soda, 1/2 teaspoon salt

### Instructions

1. Line a slow cooker with parchment paper, slightly greased6-quarters.
2. In a medium bowl, combine flour, maize meal, baking powder, baking soda, and salt. Set aside.
3. Beat butter and sugar with an electric mixer until smooth, about 2 minutes.
4. Add eggs and beat 2 minutes more.
5. Mixing sour cream, lemon zest, vanilla extract, and poppy seeds with the mixer on low.
6. Add the flour mixture slowly, then mix well.
7. For 2 hours 15 minutes to 2 hours 30 minutes, pour batter into the parchment-lined slow cooker — cover and cook on warm. The cake should be placed in the middle.

8. Remove cover and turn off the crockpot.
9. Whisk together lemon juice and pastry sugar in a small bowl.
10. That's right. Remove from the crockpot insert and place it on a wire rack to cool. Drizzle the mixture of lemon/sugar on top.

**Serving** - 6

**Prep Time** – 10 min

**Macros** - Calories: 339kcal

## 124. KEY LIME DUMP CAKE RECIPE

### Ingredients

- 15.25 oz. Betty Crocker French Vanilla Cake Mix box
- 44 oz. Key Lime Pie Filling {2 cans 22 oz. each}
- 8 tbsp. or 1/2 cup Butter melted {1 stick}

### Instructions

1. Spray inside the Crock-Pot with a non-stick cooking spray Empty Key Lime Pie Cans filling in the Crock-Pot bottom and then spread evenly.
2. Mix the dry vanilla cake mix with the melted butter in a large mixing bowl, then stir until crumbly. Break up any big chunks into small spoon crumbles}.
3. Pour the crumble cake/butter mixture over the Crock-Pot Key Lime mixture, spread evenly, and cover the Crock-Pot with the lid.
4. Cook for 2 hours at HIGH or 4 hours at LOW.

5. Serve with Ice Cream or Whip Cream and ENJOY.

**Prep Time** - 20 min

**Servings** - 8

**Macros**      - Calories:      280kcal      | Carbohydrates: 58g | Protein: 2g | Fat: 4g | Saturated Fat: 2g | Sugar: 41g |

## 125. CROCKPOT CARAMEL SAUCE RECIPE {DULCE DE LECHE}

### Ingredient

- 28 oz. Eagle Sweetened Condensed Milk
- 4 Full Mouth Mason Jars {8 oz. each}

### Instructions

1. Pour condensed sweetened milk into four containers evenly, leaving 1″ of space at the top of each box.
2. Solid screw lids.
3. Put the jars in the Crockpot, then fill the Crockpot with warm water until the jars are completely submerged, with about 1″ extra water over the jar lids.
4. Cook for 9 hours at LOW.
5. Remove jars with tongs after 9 hours carefully and allow to cool for 30 minutes.
6. Remove the lids after the jars have cooled, grab some apple slices, and begin to dip into your delicious caramel sauce!

**Prep Time** - 5 min

**Servings** - 4

**Macros** - Calories: 91kcal | Carbohydrates: 15g | Protein: 2g | Fat: 2g | Saturated Fat: 1g | Potassium: 105mg | Sugar: 15g

## 126. CROCKPOT CHERRY DUMP CAKE RECIPE

### Ingredients

- 15.25 oz. Betty Crocker Devil's Food Cake Mix
- 42 oz. Cherry Pie Filling {2 cans 21 oz. each}
- 1/2 cup Butter melted {8 Tbsp. or 113 grams}

### Instructions

1. Spray with non-stick cooking spray
2. 2 inside the Crockpot.
3. Empty Cherry Pie Filling cans into Crockpot's bottom, then evenly spread out.
4. Combine dry cake mix with melted butter in a medium mixing bowl and stir until crumbly. Break up some big chunks into small spoon crumbles}.
5. Pour the crumble cake/butter mixture over the Crockpot cherries, scatter evenly, and cover the Crockpot with a lid.
6. Cook for 2 hours at HIGH, or 4 hours at LOW. Use Ice Cream or Whip Cream to serve. ENJOY!!

**Prep Time** - 5 mins

**Servings** - 8

**Macros** - Calories 566, Fat 17g, Saturated Fat 11g, Carbohydrates 98g, Fiber 1g, Sugar 37g, Protein 3g

## 127. CROCKPOT PUMPKIN SPICE CAKE RECIPE

### Ingredients

- 15.25 oz. Betty Crocker Spice Cake Mix {1 box}
- 15 oz. Libby's Pure Pumpkin {1 can}
- ½ cup Applesauce
- Three eggs
- 1 tsp. Pumpkin Pie Spice

### Instructions

1. Beat all the ingredients together with a mixer for 1 minute.
2. Spray with Nonstick Cooking Spray inside the Crockpot.
3. Pour over and cover the mixture into the Crockpot.
4. Cook for 1.5 – 2 hours or until finished.
5. I just cut pieces directly out of the Crockpot carefully once the cake was made.

**Prep Time** - 5 min

**Servings** - 8

**Macros** - Total NET CARBS 4.42 g, Calories: 344kcal, Total fat: 30.38g, Carbohydrate: 10.03g, Fiber: 5.61g, Protein: 8.26g

## 128. CROCKPOT BLUEBERRY DUMP CAKE RECIPE

### Ingredients

- 15.25 oz. Betty Crocker Lemon Cake Mix {1 box}
- 42 oz. Blueberry Pie Filling {2 cans 21 oz. each}
- 1/2 cup Butter melted {8 Tbsp.}

### Instructions

1. Spray with non-stick cooking spray.

2. The Crockpot's back. Blueberry Pie Filling empty cans and spread evenly into the bottom of Crockpot.
3. In a mixing bowl, combine dry Lemon Cake Mix with melted butter and stir until crumbly. Break some big chunks into the crumbles of a small spoon.
4. Pour the crumble cake/butter mixture over the blueberry mixture into Crockpot, spread evenly, and cover with a lid the crockpot.
5. Cook at HIGH for 2 hours, and at LOW for 4 hours.
6. Serve with Ice Cream, and Whip Cream ENJOY!!

**Prep Time** - 5 min

**Servings** - 8

**Macros** - Total NET CARBS 4.42 g, Calories: 344kcal, Total fat: 30.38g, Carbohydrate: 10.03g, Fiber: 5.61g, Protein: 8.26g

# 129. CROCKPOT STRAWBERRY DUMP CAKE RECIPE

## Ingredients

- 15.25 oz. Betty Crocker Strawberry Cake Mix {1 box}
- 42 oz. Strawberry Pie Filling {2 cans 21 oz. each}
- 1/2 cup butter melted

## Instructions

1. Spray with a non-stick cooking spray inside the Crockpot.
2. Strawberry Pie Filling empty cans into Crockpot's bottom and spread evenly.

3. Combine dry cake mix with melted butter butter butter in a medium mixing bowl and stir until crumbly. Break up some big chunks into small spoon crumbles}.
4. Pour the cake/butter crumbled mixture into Crockpot over strawberries and spread evenly, covering the crockpot with a lid.
5. Cook for 2 hours at HIGH, or 4 hours at LOW.
6. Using Ice Cream or Whip Cream to drink. ALWAYS!!

**Prep TIme** - 5 min

**Servings** - 8

**Macros** - Total NET CARBS 4.42 g, Calories: 344kcal, Total fat: 30.38g, Carbohydrate: 10.03g, Fiber: 5.61g, Protein: 8.26g

# 130. CROCKPOT RED VELVET CAKE

## Ingredient

- ½ cup of Applesauce
- 1⅓ cup of Water
- 3 Eggs
- 15.25 ounces of Duncan Hines Red Velvet Cake Mix {1 box}

## Instructions

1. For 1 minute, combine all ingredients with a mixer.
2. Spray with Pam Cooking Spray inside Crockpot.
3. Pour over and cover the mixture into the Crockpot.
4. Cook for 1.5–2 hours or until done at medium.

5. Once the cake has been made, I just cut pieces out of the Crockpot carefully.
6. Enjoy adding some of your favorite frostings, as well!
7. Serve with ENJOY and ice cream!!

**Prep TIme** - 15 mins

**Servings** - 12

**Macros** - Calories 380, Total Fat 17g, Saturated Fat 5g, Total Carbohydrate 54g

## 131. CROCKPOT BAKED APPLES RECIPE

### Ingredients

- Five medium Gala apple {depending on the size of your Crockpot}
- ½ cup Quaker Old Fashioned Oats
- ½ cup Brown Sugar
- 3 tsp. Cinnamon
- 1 tsp. Allspice
- 1/4 cup butter

### Instructions

1. Pour 1/4 cup of water at Crockpot's edge.
2. Use a sharp knife to carefully core apples.
3. Then use the edge of a knife to peel around the top about — 1/2 inch peel.
4. Mix the oats, cinnamon, brown sugar, and allspice.
5. Fill a single apple with a mixture of Oats / Sugar / Spice.
6. Use a butter pat to top each apple.
7. Set in Crockpot carefully and put the lid on Crockpot.
8. Cook for 3–4 hours or until finished. ENJOY!

**Prep Time** - 15 min

**Servings** - 6

**Macros** - Fat 3g, Carbohydrates 48g, Fiber 5g, Sugar 36g, Protein 1g.

# SIDE DISHES RECIPES

## 132. BUTTER-FRIED GREEN CABBAGE

### Ingredients

- 1½ lbs shredded green cabbage
- 3 oz. unsalted butter
- salt and pepper

### Instructions

1. Use a food processor, mandolin slicer, or a sharp knife to cut the cabbage.
2. Place over medium heat a large skillet. Stir in milk.
3. Remove the cabbage and sauté, occasionally stirring, for at least 15 minutes, until the cabbage is wilted and golden brown around the edges.
4. Lower the heat slightly to the edge—to taste salt and pepper.

**Macros** - Net carbs: (6 g), Fiber: 4 g, Fat: (17 g), Protein: (2 g), kcal: 193

**Prep Time** 25 mins

**Servings** 4

## 133. COLESLAW RECIPE

### Ingredients

- ½ lb green cabbage
- ½ lemon, the juice
- 1 tsp salt, 1 tbsp Dijon mustard
- ½cup mayonnaise or vegan mayonnaise
- One pinch fennel seeds (optional), One pinch pepper

### Instructions

1. Use a food processor, mandolin or sharp cheese slicer to cut the core and shred the cabbage.
2. Place the chicken in a bowl of medium size.
3. Add lemon juice and salt.
4. To allow the cabbage to wilt slightly, stir and let sit for 10 minutes. Discard any liquid waste.
5. Mix the cabbage, mayonnaise, and mustard as an alternative.
6. Taste the season.

**Macros** - Net carbs: (3 g), Fiber: 2 g, Fat: (21 g), Protein: (1 g), kcal: 209

**Prep time** 15 mins

**Servings** 4

## 134. BROCCOLI AND CAULIFLOWER IN CHEESE

### Ingredients

- ½ lb cauliflower, chopped
- 1 lb broccoli, chopped
- 3 oz. Leeks, 5 oz. Shredded cheese, 3 oz. butter
- 4 tbsp sour cream
- ½ cup fresh oregano or fresh thyme
- salt and pepper

### Instructions

1. Cut all vegetables into bits of bite-size.
2. Place a large skillet in medium-high heat and fry the vegetables in butter to a golden brown.

3. Remove remaining ingredients and stir to taste until the cheese is melted.

**Macros** - Net carbs: (9 g) Fiber: 5 g Fat: (31 g) Protein: (14 g)kcal: 367

**Prep Time** 20 mins

**Servings** 4

# 135. ROASTED FENNEL AND SNOW PEA SALAD

## Ingredients

- 1 lb fresh fennel
- 3 tbsp olive oil, sea salt
- One lemon, ground black pepper
- 2 tbsp of pumpkin seeds, toasted
- 5 oz. snow peas

## Instructions

1. Heat the oven up to 225 ° C (450 ° F).
2. Cut off the fennel the stalks and fronds. Then cut into small wedges, the fennel bulb. Set aside in a baking dish. Add olive oil to the top. To taste the salt and the pepper.
3. Half the lemon and squeeze the juice out. Cut the lemon into thin wedges and then put it around the fennel.
4. Bake for 20–30 minutes in the oven or until a beautiful golden color has transformed into the fennel.
5. While baking the fennel, place the seeds of the pumpkin in a dry frying pan and toast for a few minutes over medium heat until browned but not burnt.
6. Mix the roasted fennel and the dry toasted pumpkin seeds with the raw shredded snow peas. Plate with fish, chicken or meat and serve.

**Macros** - Net carbs: (8 g) Fiber: 5 g Fat: (12 g) Protein: (4 g) kcal: 165

**Prep Time** 40 mins

**Servings** 4

# 136. BAKED MINI BELL PEPPERS

## Ingredients

- 8 oz. mini bell peppers, about 2 per serving
- 1 oz. air-dried chorizo, finely chopped
- 1 tbsp fresh thyme, finely chopped or fresh cilantro
- 8 oz. cream cheese, 4 oz. shredded cheese
- ½ tbsp of mild chipotle paste, 2 tbsp of olive oil

## Instructions

1. Set the oven at 200 ° C (325 ° F). Lengthwise break the peppers of the bell and remove the core.
2. Cut the chorizo and herbs perfect.
3. In a small bowl, combine the cream cheese, spices, and oil. Add the herbs and chorizo. Disable to smooth.
4. Fill the mixture with the bell peppers and put in a deep baking dish.
5. Sprinkle on top of shredded cheese. Bake for like 15–20 minutes until golden brown and the cheese is melted.

**Macros** - Net carbs: (6 g) Fiber: 1 g Fat: (37 g) Protein: (12 g) kcal: 412

**Prep time** 35 mins

**Servings** 4

## 137. LOW-CARB CAULIFLOWER RICE

### Ingredients

- 1½ lbs cauliflower
- ½ tsp salt
- ½ tsp turmeric (optional)
- 3 oz. butter or coconut oil

### Instructions

1. Shred the whole head of the cauliflower using a grater or grater attachment on a food processor.
2. Melt in a pan butter or coconut oil. Remove the cauliflower and cook for 5-10 minutes over medium heat or until a little softened by the riced cauliflower.
3. During frying, add salt and the optional turmeric.

**Macros** - Net carbs: (5 g) Fiber: 3 g Fat: (18 g) Protein: (3 g) kcal: 193

**Prep Time** 20 mins

**Servings** 4

## 138. LOW-CARB CAULIFLOWER HASH BROWNS

### Ingredients

- 1 lb cauliflower
- Three eggs
- ½ yellow onion, grated
- 1 tsp salt
- Two pinches pepper
- 4 oz. butter, for frying

### Instructions

1. Use a food processor or grater to clean, cut, and grate the cauliflower.
2. Add a large bowl of cauliflower. Remove the rest of the ingredients and blend together. Set 5–10 minutes aside.
3. Melt a generous quantity of butter or oil in a large skillet over medium heat. When you intend to have space for 3–4 pancakes (approximately 3–4 inches each) at a time, the cooking process will go faster. Use the low heat oven to keep the pancakes ' first lots hot while you're making the others.
4. Place the rubbed cauliflower scoops in the frying pan and carefully flatten them until they are about 3–4 inches in diameter.
5. Fry on both sides for 4–5 minutes. To make sure they don't burn, adjust the heat.

**Macros** - Net carbs: (5 g) Fiber: 3 g Fat: (26 g) Protein: (7 g) kcal: 282

**Prep Time** 40 mins

**Servings** 4

## 139. OVEN-ROASTED BRUSSELS SPROUTS WITH PARMESAN CHEESE

### Ingredients

- 1½ lbs Brussels sprouts
- 3 tbsp olive oil
- 1 tsp dried rosemary or dried thyme
- salt and pepper
- 3 oz. shaved parmesan cheese

### Instructions

1. Heat the oven up to 225 ° C (450 ° F).

2. Trim the sprouts from Brussels and cut them in half.
3. Layer in a baking dish and pour over olive oil. Add rosemary/thyme and salt and pepper.
4. Roast for 15–20 minutes in the oven or until the sprouts in Brussels turned a beautiful color. Shave and enjoy parmesan cheese!

**Macros** - Net carbs: (9 g) Fiber: 7 g Fat: (16 g) Protein: (13 g) kcal: 245

**Prep Time** 30 mins

**Servings** 4

## 140. ZUCCHINI FETTUCCINE

### Ingredients

- One zucchini
- 1 oz. olive oil or butter
- salt and pepper

### Instructions

1. Prepare for approximately one zucchini of medium size per male.
2. Divide the zucchini lengthwise in half.
3. With a knife, scoop the seeds and cut the halves with a potato peeler rather thinly or use a spiralizer to make zoodles.
4. In a simmering sauce of your choosing, mix the zucchini noodles, and serve immediately.
5. If you don't use a sauce to eat your zucchini, boil half a gallon (a few liters) of salted water in a large pot and parboil the slices of zucchini for one minute.

6. Drain the water and stir and serve with olive oil or butter— salt and pepper.

**Macros** - Net carbs: 9 % (7 g) Fiber: 3 g Fat: 86 % (29 g)nProtein: 5 % (4 g) kcal: 302

**Prep Time** 15 mins

**Servings** 1

## 141. BROWNED BUTTER CAULIFLOWER MASH

### Ingredients

- Two yellow onions, finely chopped
- 3 tbsp butter, for frying
- 3 lbs cauliflower
- 1½ cups heavy whipping cream
- 10 oz. shredded cheddar cheese
- 1 tsp sea salt
- ½ tsp ground black pepper
- 6 oz. butter

### Instructions

1. In a generous amount of butter, fry the chopped onions until soft and golden. Put it aside.
2. Shred the cauliflower with a grater's coarse side, or split it into smaller florets until it is rice-sized and chop in a food processor. Filter at a time a few florets.
3. Pour heavy cream into a saucepan. Add the rice of the cauliflower and cook over medium heat. Let it cook for 10–15 minutes or more until the cauliflower is cooked thoroughly, and the cream is through. This will add a neutral flavor to the mash.

4. To taste the salt and the pepper. Add the onion fried and the cheese shredded. Mix well and stay warm.
5. Melt the butter for a soft, nutty taste at medium heat in a skillet until amber-colored. Serve the melted butter.

**Macros** - Net carbs: 7 % (10 g) Fiber: 4 g Fat: 83 % (49 g) Protein: 10 % (13 g) kcal: 534

**Prep time** 35

**Servings** 8

## 142. CREAMED GREEN CABBAGE

### Ingredients

- 2 oz. butter
- 1½ lbs green cabbage
- 1¼ cups heavy whipping cream
- salt and pepper
- ½ cup fresh parsley, finely chopped
- 1 tbsp lemon zest

### Instructions

1. Begin by using a food processor to shred the cabbage or cut it thinly with a sharp knife.
2. Melt the butter over medium-high heat in a frying pan. Remove the cabbage and sauté around the edges for a couple of minutes until soft and golden brown.
3. Add heavy cream to the whipping and boil until the cream is reduced. Reduce heat to the limit.
4. To taste the salt and the pepper.
5. Until eating, add parsley and lemon zest.

**Macros** - Net carbs: 8 % (8 g) Fiber: 5 g Fat: 87 % (38 g) Protein: 5 % (5 g) kcal: 398

**Prep Time** 20 mins

**Servings** 4

## 143. LOW-CARB CAULIFLOWER MASH

### Ingredients

- 1 lb cauliflower
- 3 oz. grated parmesan cheese
- 4 oz. butter
- ½ lemon, juice, and zest
- olive oil (optional)

### Instructions

1. Cut into florets the cauliflower.
2. Boil the cauliflower in plenty of slightly salted water for a few minutes – just enough, so the florets are soft, but keep a somewhat firm texture. Strain the cauliflower in a colander and drain the water.
3. Attach the cauliflower with the remaining ingredients to a food processor and pulse until consistency is desired. You can also use a blender for immersion.
4. To taste salt and pepper. If you want to add more olive oil or butter.

**Macros** - Net carbs: 6 % (5 g) Fiber: 2 g Fat: 82 % (28 g) Protein: 13 % (10 g) kcal: 313

**Prep time** 20 mins

**Servings** 4

## 144. OVEN-BAKED RUTABAGA WEDGES

### Ingredients

- 1 lb rutabaga
- ¼ cup olive oil
- 1 tsp chili powder or paprika powder
- salt and pepper

### Instructions

1. Preheat the oven to a 200 ° C temperature.
2. Rinse the rutabagas and peel them. Smaller roots in the oven are going to bake quicker.
3. Break into wedges and spread over a sheet of baking.
4. Salt and potatoes. Sprinkle on top of olive oil and blend well.
5. Place in the oven and bake until the wedges turn a beautiful color for 20 minutes. Use a knife to test for readiness. They cook towards the end quicker, so be careful.
6. Serve with your favorite meat or fish.

**Macros** - Net carbs: 18 % (7 g) Fiber: 3 g Fat: 79 % (14 g) Protein: 3 % (1 g) kcal: 167

**Prep time** 25 mins

**Servings** 4

## 145. CREAMY LEMON GREEN BEANS

### Ingredients

- 10 oz. fresh green beans
- 3 oz. butter or olive oil
- ½ tsp sea salt
- ¼ tsp ground black pepper
- 1 cup heavy whipping cream

- ½ lemon, the zest
- ½ cup fresh parsley (optional)

### Instructions

1. Trim the green beans and rinse them.
2. In a frying pan, heat butter or oil.
3. Sauté the beans over medium-high heat for 3-4 minutes until they start to brown. Reduce the temperature to the maximum— to taste salt and pepper.
4. Remove heavy cream and cook for 1-2 minutes. Apply the lemon zest thinly and sprinkle before serving on the green beans.
5. Until serving, add the finely chopped parsley.

**Macros** - Net carbs: 5 % (5 g) Fiber: 2 g Fat: 91 % (39 g) Protein: 3 % (3 g) kcal: 376

**Prep time** 25 mins

**Servings** 4

## 146. CAPRESE SNACK

### Ingredients

- 8 oz. cherry tomatoes
- 8 oz. mozzarella, mini cheese balls
- 2 tbsp green pesto
- salt and pepper

### Instructions

1. Split into half the tomatoes and balls of mozzarella. Remove and blend the pesto.
2. To taste the salt and the pepper.

**Macros** - Net carbs: 6 % (3 g) Fiber: 1 g Fat: 69 % (17 g) Protein: 25 % (14 g) kcal: 218

**Prep Time** 5 mins

Servings 4

## 147. LOW-CARB EGGPLANT HASH WITH EGGS

### Ingredients

- One yellow onion, finely chopped
- 2 tbsp olive oil
- ½ lb halloumi cheese, diced into small cubes
- Two eggplants, diced
- salt and pepper
- Four eggs
- 2 tbsp butter
- ½ tsp Worcestershire sauce (optional)

### Instructions

1. In medium heat, fry the onion in the oil until soft.
2. Add eggplant and halloumi cheese and fry until all is dark golden — salt and pepper to taste.
3. Fry the eggs in a different pan as you like them and serve with a few drops of Worcestershire sauce (optional).

**Macros** - Net carbs: 11 % (11 g) Fiber: 8 g Fat: 69 % (31 g) Protein: 20 % (20 g) kcal: 425

**Prep Time** 20 mins

**Servings** 4

## 148. BRUSSELS SPROUTS WITH CARAMELIZED RED ONIONS

### Ingredients

- One red onion
- 4 oz. butter
- 1 tbsp red wine vinegar
- salt and pepper
- 1 lb Brussels sprouts

### Instructions

1. Divide the onions into wedges and fry for 5–10 minutes in half of the butter over medium heat.
2. The onions are supposed to turn golden but not burnt. Apply to taste the vinegar, salt, and pepper.
3. Lower the heat, when stirring, and start to sauté the onion. Place yourself on a plate.
4. Sprouts the Brussels rinse and trim and cut them in half. You can fry them all if they're tiny.
5. Fry the Brussels sprouts with more butter in the same frying pan until a beautiful color and a little soft has been transformed. Search with a knife or a stick. "Al dente" is best served to them.
6. Salt and potatoes. Remove and mix the onions.

**Macros** - Net carbs: 12 % (8 g) Fiber: 5 g Fat: 81 % (23 g) Protein: 7 % (4 g) kcal: 261

**Prep Time** 30mins

**Servings** 4

## 149. KETO STUFFED MUSHROOMS

### Ingredients

- 8 oz. bacon
- 12 mushrooms
- 2 tbsp butter, 3 tbsp fresh chives, finely chopped, 1 tsp paprika powder
- 7 oz. cream cheese
- salt and pepper

## Instructions

1. Preheat the oven to a 200 ° C temperature.
2. Begin by frying the bacon until it's crispy. Let the crumbs cool and crumble. Save the meat from the bacon.
3. Cut the stems of the mushroom and finely chop them. In the bacon fat, add butter if necessary.
4. In a greased baking dish, put the mushrooms.
5. Mix the crumbled bacon in a bowl with the fried, chopped stems of the mushroom and the other ingredients. Attach to each mushroom some of the mixes.
6. Bake until the mushrooms turn golden brown for 20 minutes.

**Macros** - Net carbs: 4 % (5 g) Fiber: 1 g Fat: 86 % (46 g) Protein: 10 % (12 g) kcal: 477

**Prep time** 40mins

**Servings** 4

## 150. ROASTED VEGETABLE TRICOLORE

### Ingredients

- 1 lb Brussels sprouts
- 8 oz. cherry tomatoes, 8 oz. mushrooms
- 1 tsp sea salt, ½ tsp ground black pepper, 1 tsp dried rosemary or dried thyme
- ½ cup olive oil

### Instructions

1. Rinse and trim all vegetables and, if necessary, peel the sprout's outer layer of the Brussels.

2. Add spices and olive oil and blend.
3. Bake for like 20 minutes or until the vegetables have softened and turned into a beautiful color.
4. Serve as a side dish with beef, chicken, or fish.

**Macros** - Net carbs: 11 % (6 g) Fiber: 4 g Fat: 81 % (18 g) Protein: 8 % (4 g) kcal: 208

**Prep Time** - 40mins

**Servings** 6

## 151. LOW-CARB BROCCOLI MASH

### Ingredients

- 1½ lbs of broccoli
- 4 tbsp of fresh basil or fresh parsley, finely chopped
- 3 oz. butter
- One garlic clove
- salt and pepper

### Instructions

1. Make sure you cut the broccoli into florets, peel, and cut into small pieces. Boil the broccoli for a couple of minutes in plenty of slightly salted water—just enough to retain a firm texture. Filter the heat.
2. Mix in a food processor with the other ingredients or use an immersion blender.
3. To taste the salt and the pepper.
4. If you like, add more oil or butter.
5. Serve hot tubes!

**Macros** - Net carbs: 14 % (7 g) Fiber: 4 g Fat: 76 % (18 g) Protein: 10 % (5 g) kcal: 210

**Prep time** 15mins

**Servings** 4

## 152. RUTABAGA CURLS

### Ingredients

- 1½ lbs rutabaga
- ⅓ cup olive oil
- 1 tbsp paprika powder or chili powder
- 1 tsp salt

### Instructions

1. Heat the oven up to 225 ° C (450 ° F). Peel and slice the rutabaga into bits you can pass through your spiralizer. Cut with scissors the long spirals to make the curls bite-sized. If you don't have a spiralizer, you can use a sharp knife to cut the root into super-thin sticks.
2. Place it in a plastic bowl or jar. Pour over the remaining ingredients and vigorously stir/shake.
3. Place on a baking sheet and bake 10 minutes in the oven. Serve immediately with your choice of main course and sauce.

**Macros** - Net carbs: 20 % (11 g) Fiber: 5 g Fat: 76 % (18 g) Protein: 4 % (2 g) kcal: 227

**Prep time** 30mins

**Servings** 4

## 153. THAI CURRY CABBAGE

### Ingredients

- 3 tbsp coconut oil
- 1 tbsp red curry paste preferably Thai
- 2 lbs shredded green cabbage
- 1 tsp salt

- 1 tbsp sesame oil

### Instructions

1. Heat the coconut oil at high heat in a frying pan over. Attach the paste of curry and whisk for a minute. Add the colt.
2. Sauce until the cob starts turning golden brown, but it's still a little chewy. Remove thoroughly and reduce heat to the limit.
3. To taste the oil. Add an additional 1–2 minutes of sesame oil and sauté and drink!

**Macros** - Net carbs: 19 % (8 g) Fiber: 6 g Fat: 73 % (14 g) Protein: 8 % (3 g) kcal: 181

**Prep Time** 30 mins

**Servings** 4

## 154. LOW-CARB ZUCCHINI AND WALNUT SALAD

### Ingredients

### Dressing

- 2 tbsp olive oil, ¾cup mayonnaise or vegan mayonnaise
- 2 tsp lemon juice, One garlic clove, finely minced
- ½ tsp salt, ¼ tsp chili powder

### Salad

- One head of Romaine lettuce
- 4 oz. of arugula lettuce ¼ cup of finely chopped fresh chives or scallions
- Two zucchini, 1 tbsp olive oil
- Salt and pepper, 3½ oz. chopped walnuts or pecans

## Instructions

1. Mix the ingredients together in a small dressing pan.
2. Cut the salad and cut it. Place the Romaine in a large bowl with arugula and chives.
3. Lengthwise break the zucchini and pick out the seeds. Cut half of the zucchini in quarter-inch sections.
4. In a frying pan, flame olive oil over medium heat until shimmering. Attach the zucchini to the container and use salt and pepper to season. Fry until lightly browned, but solid.
5. In the salad, add the cooked zucchini and blend.
6. In the same pan as the zucchini, roast the nuts briefly. Coat on a salad with salt and pepper spoon nuts and chop with salad dressing.

**Macros** - Net carbs: 6 % (8 g) Fiber: 7 g Fat: 88 % (58 g) Protein: 6 % (9 g) kcal: 595

**Prep time** 35 min

**Servings** 4

## 155. LOW-CARB CAULIFLOWER CHEESE

### Ingredient

- 1 lb of frozen or fresh broccoli, cut into florets
- 1 cup of heavy whipping cream
- 2 oz. of butter
- 7 oz. cream cheese
- salt and pepper
- 2 tsp of garlic powder
- 1¾ lbs cauliflower, cut into small florets
- 8 oz. shredded cheese

## Instructions

1. Preheat the oven at 180 ° C (350 ° F).
2. Place flowers of broccoli in a bowl. Add water and bring to a boil until sealed. Cook until fork-tender is broccoli.
3. When finished, strain the broccoli and discard the water, add the cream cheese, heavy whipping cream, butter, salt, pepper, and garlic powder with an immersion blender to the pot and puree. Remove the broccoli and puree together until smooth.
4. Grease a baking dish or 9x12 "with some butter. Remove florets of cauliflower to the baking dish.
5. Pour over the florets and cover with shredded cheese with the broccoli cream sauce. Bake, 40 minutes in the oven or until the fork-tender, is the cauliflower, and the top is golden brown.

**Macros** - Net carbs: 9 % (11 g) Fiber: 5 g Fat: 78 % (44 g) Protein: 13 % (17 g) kcal: 511

**Prep Time** 15 mins

**Servings** 6

## 156. TURNIP GRATIN

### Ingredients

- ½ yellow onion
- 1½ lbs turnip
- One garlic clove
- ½ cup fresh chives, finely chopped
- 2 oz. butter
- 1¼ cups heavy whipping cream
- 7 oz. shredded cheese
- ½ tsp salt

- ¼ tsp ground black pepper

## Instruction

1. Preheat the oven to 200 °C.
2. Peel the onion, garlic, and seasoning. Slice all very finely with a mandolin or food processor.
3. Chop the chives perfect.
4. Grease a 9 "baking dish with butter and add slices of onion, garlic and chives, and most cheese, save some on top— salt and pepper to taste.
5. Add cream and remaining cheese on top. Bake until bubbly and golden brown for about 30 minutes.

**Macros** - Net carbs: 8 % (8 g) Fiber: 2 g Fat: 81 % (35 g) Protein: 11 % (11 g) kcal: 387

**Prep time** 15 mins

**Servings** 6

## 157. EASY WHITE TURKEY CHILI

### Ingredients

- 1 lb Organic ground turkey (or ground beef, lamb or pork)
- 2 cups riced cauliflower, 2 cups full-fat coconut milk (or heavy cream)
- 2 tbsp. coconut oil
- 1/2 a Vidalia onion
- Two garlic cloves
- 1 tbsp. mustard, 1 tsp of salt, black pepper, thyme, celery salt, garlic powder

### Instructions

1. Heat the coconut oil in a large bowl.
2. While slim the garlic and onion. Bring it in the hot oil.

3. Stir in the ground turkey for 2-3 minutes.
4. Break with the spatula and stir until it crumbles continuously.
5. Place cauliflower and rice in the seasoning mix and stir well.
6. Add the coconut milk once the meat is browned, bring it to a simmer and reduce for 5-8 minutes, stirring frequently.
7. It's ready to serve at this stage. Or you can cause it to shrink by half and act as a dip.
8. For an extra thick sauce, mix in shredded cheese.

**Macros** - Calories: 388 kcal   Fat: 30.5g Carbohydrates: 5.5g Protein: 28.8g

**Servings** 5

**Prep time** 5mins

## 158. BALSAMIC ROASTED TURNIPS

### Ingredients

- Three turnips
- 2 tbsp balsamic vinaigrette
- 1 tbsp garlic

### Instructions

1. Heat the oven up to 400.
2. Peel and cut into cubes.
3. Combine turnips, 2 tbsp of balsamic dressing, and garlic in a bowl.
4. Place the turnips on a parchment paper-lined baking sheet.
5. Bake for 30 minutes at 400 or until browning begins.

**Serving Size**: 1 cup

**Macros**       Calories: 32       Fat: 0g
Carbohydrates: Net Carbs: 7g Fiber: 3g
Protein: 1g

**Prep time** 10 mins

**Servings** 3

## 159. CRISPY KALE CHIPS

### Ingredients

- 2 cups kale (this recipe uses dino/Tuscan kale, but any type will suffice)
- 2 tbsp Himalayan sea salt
- Avocado oil spray

### Instructions

1. Oven preheats to 350 degrees.
2. Cut the kale and spread it on a parchment paper-lined baking sheet.
3. Spray the avocado oil spray kale.
4. Coat with the Himalayan sea salt 2 tbsp.
5. Bake 15-20 minutes or till it is crispy.

**Macros** - Serving Size: 1 cup Fat: 0g
Carbohydrates: Net Carbs: 3g Fiber: 2g
Protein: 2g

**Prep time** 3mins

**Servings** 2

## 160. CREAMY TURNIP KETO "MASHED POTATOES" WITH BACON

### Ingredients

- Four large turnips
- 1/2 cup bacon bits
- 2 TBSP grass-fed butter
- 1/2 cup almond milk

### Instructions

1. Peel, clean, and cut into cubes the turnips.
2. Place in a saucepan and then fill with water.
3. Bring water to a boil and simmer until tender for 12-15 minutes.
4. Cooked turnips strain and rinse.
5. Place in a large mixing bowl and break turnips into smaller bits using a fork.
6. Combine all the ingredients with a hand blender or other form of a mixer.
7. Provide milk and butter for the almond. Mix together with the desired consistency. Attach to taste salt and pepper.

**Macros** - Serving Size: 1 cup Fat: 7g
Carbohydrates: Net Carbs: 3g Fiber: 1g
Protein: 1g

**Prep time** 10mins

## 161. CRISPY ROASTED EGGPLANT CHIPS

### Ingredients

- 1/4 cup olive oil
- 1 Large eggplant (thinly sliced)
- 1/2 teaspoon salt
- 1/4 teaspoon pepper
- One teaspoon garlic powder
- 1/2 teaspoon dried basil
- 1/2 teaspoon dried oregano
- 1/4 cup parmesan cheese

### Instructions

1. Preheat the oven to 325 ° C.

2. Add 1/4 cup extra virgin olive oil and dried spices in a small bowl. Coat with the oil and spices on the sliced eggplant. Set them up on a baking tray.
3. Bake until the chips are evenly browned for about 15-20 minutes. Flip over the baking time 1/2. If needed, remove from the oven and sprinkle with parmesan cheese. Eventually, let it cool to serve.

**Macros** - Serving Size: 1 chip Calories: 60 Fat: 5g  Carbohydrates: Net  Carbs:  2g Protein: 1g

**Prep time** 10 mins

**Servings** 15

## 162. LOW-CARB CABBAGE CASSEROLE

### Ingredients

- 2 lbs green cabbage
- One yellow onion
- Two garlic cloves
- 4 oz. butter
- 1½ cups heavy whipping cream
- 6 tbsp sour cream or crème fraîche
- 6 oz. cream cheese
- 1 tbsp ranch seasoning
- ½ tsp ground black pepper
- 1 tsp salt
- 6 oz. shredded cheese

### Instructions

1. Preheat the oven to 200 ° C. Use a sharp knife or mandolin slicer to cut onion, garlic, and green cabbage.
2. Heat and add the butter to a large frying pan. Sauté the vegetables for about 8-10 minutes until softened.

Remove milk, sour cream, cheese with butter and spices. Remove thoroughly and allow another 5–10 minutes to simmer.
3. Add to a baking dish. Sprinkle the cheese on top and bake till the cheese melts and turns golden for 20 minutes.

**Macros** - Net carbs: 7 % (11 g) Fiber: 4 g Fat: 84 % (57 g) Protein: 8 % (13 g) kcal: 612

**Prep Time** 15 mins

**Servings** 6

## 163. ROASTED CABBAGE

### Ingredients

- 2 lbs green cabbage
- 6 oz. butter
- 1 tsp salt
- ¼ tsp ground black pepper

### Instructions

1. Preheat the oven to 200 ° C.
2. Melt the butter with medium-low heat in a casserole.
3. Divide the green cabbage into wedges and cut in the middle of the thick stem. Cut slices - less than one inch thick and place in a large baking dish or on a baking sheet lined with parchment paper.
4. Add pepper, salt, and pour over the melted butter.
5. Bake till the cabbage is roasted for 20 minutes.

**Macros** - Net carbs: 8 % (8 g) Fiber: 6 g Fat: 88 % (35 g) Protein: 4 % (3 g) kcal: 365

**Prep time** 10 mins

**Servings** 4

## 164. LOW-CARB TORTILLAS

### Ingredients

- Two eggs
- Two egg whites
- 5 oz. cream cheese
- 1½ tsp ground psyllium husk powder
- 1 tbsp coconut flour
- ½ tsp salt

### Instructions

1. Preheat the oven to 200 ° C.
2. Beat the white eggs and bacon until smooth. Continue to beat, preferably for a few minutes, with a hand mixer. Add cream cheese and mix until a smooth batter.
3. In a small bowl, add oil, psyllium husk, and coconut flour. Add one spoonful of the flour mixture to the butter and mix well. Let the batter sit for a couple of minutes, like a pancake batter, until it gets thick. How fast the swelling of the mixture depends on the psyllium husk powder brand— some trial and error may be required.
4. Take out two sheets of baking and put on each parchment paper. Using a spatula, distribute the batter thinly into 4–6 circles or two rectangles (not more than ¼ inch thick).
5. Bake for about 5 minutes or more on the upper rack until the tortilla turns around the edges a little yellow. Carefully check the bottom side to prevent it from burning.
6. Serve with your choice of filling. We love them with beef and salsa tex-mixed ground! So cheese is a winner all the time.

Macros - Net carbs: 6 % (2 g) Fiber: 1 g Fat: 78 % (10 g) Protein: 17 % (5 g) kcal: 116

**Prep Time** 5mins

**Servings** 6

## 165. LOW-CARB STUFFING

### Ingredients

- 2 tbsp butter
- Two yellow onions, finely chopped
- 5 oz. bacon, diced
- 8 oz. celery root, diced
- One apple, grated
- 2 oz. pecans, chopped
- Two buns or slices of low-carb bread
- 1 cup heavy whipping cream
- 2 lbs ground pork
- fresh sage 2-3 sprigs, finely chopped
- ½ tsp ground nutmeg
- 1 tsp salt
- ½ tsp ground black pepper
- 1 tbsp butter

### Instruction

1. Preheat the oven at 175 ° C. The recipe is going to make enough to stuff the turkey and bake in the oven for a side dish.
2. In oil, ghee, lard or duck fat, brown onions, bacon, and celery root until golden.
3. Stir in the sage's two-thirds (save the remainder for garnish), plus all the grated apple and pecans. Extract from it and let it cool.
4. Crumble or split the low-carb bread slices in a large bowl and pour over the heavy cream. Let a little swell the rice.

5. Attach the ground beef, spices, and the mixture of brown onion and garlic. Toss it, but don't overdo it. It shouldn't be too uniform or lightweight for objects.
6. Put in a grated baking dish and bake for 25–30 minutes in the oven or until the meat is cooked thoroughly.
7. Garnish and serve on your Thanksgiving table with new sage leaves.

**Macros** - Net carbs: 6 % (8 g) Fiber: 2 g Fat: 76 % (46 g) Protein: 18 % (25 g) kcal: 543

**Prep Time** 20mins

**Servings** 8

## 166. PARMESAN-ROASTED GREEN BEANS

### Ingredients

- One egg
- 2 tbsp olive oil
- 1 tsp onion powder
- ½ tsp salt
- ¼ tsp pepper
- 1 lb fresh green beans
- 1 oz. parmesan cheese, grated

### Instructions

1. Preheat to 200 ° C in the oven. Whisk together eggs, butter, and spices in a pan. Remove the beans and stir until all the green beans are covered by the egg batter.
2. Remove excess fluid and stir vigorously with the parmesan cheese.
3. Place the beans on a parchment paper-lined baking sheet. Bake for

15–20 minutes at the upper level in the oven or until the beans turn a beautiful color.

**Prep Time** 10mins

**Servings** 4

## 167. CRANBERRY SAUCE

### Ingredients

- 12 oz fresh cranberries
- Zest medium orange
- 1 tsp stevia
- 1/2 tsp vanilla extract
- 3/4 cup water

### Instructions

1. In a casserole, add all ingredients and bring to the boil.
2. Reduce heat and cook 15 minutes.
3. Nice for 4 hours.
4. Serve as cold as possible.

**Macros** - Calories: 27 Fat: 0.1g Carbohydrates: 7.2g (4.5g net) Protein: 0.3g

**Servings** 6

**Prep time** 30mins

## 168. BROWN BUTTER BUFFALO BITES

### Ingredients

- One head of cauliflower (approx 3 cups of florets)
- 1/4 cup Frank's Red Hot
- 2 tbsp. Grass-Fed Butter
- Two garlic cloves
- Pinch of salt

### Instructions

1. Melt the butter and take it to low heat until browned.
2. At that time, but in florets, your cauliflower.
3. Add a big pan.
4. Preheat the oven to 400F. Then add the garlic to the butter, and it should be almost ready.
5. When browned, cut the butter (but before it is smoked) and pour over the cauliflower. Make sure you get into the cloves of the garlic. Remove the hot sauce and swirl gently to paint.
6. To move the flowers to a sheet pan, use tongs. Set them up side by side. Save the remaining extra sauce in the pan.
7. Bake for 20 minutes the cauliflower. Move to a serving dish. Remove from the oven. Drizzle the rest of the sauce. Garnish with crispy bacon and ready for dunking with a ranch!

**Macros** - Calories: 175 Fat: 11g Carbohydrates: 10g Protein: 4g

**Prep time** 10 mins

**Servings** 2

## 169. KETO CHICKEN HEMP HEART TENDERS

### Ingredients

- 1 cup hemp hearts 1.5 pounds boneless skinless pastured chicken breast (2)
- Two large eggs
- One tablespoon apple cider vinegar
- Two tablespoon water, two tablespoons garlic powder, two tablespoons flax meal, 1 tablespoon nutritional yeast
- One teaspoon salt

### Instructions

1. Heat up to 425F in the oven.
2. Cut the breast of the chicken into tenders; make 4-5 tenders for each breast. Put it aside.
3. Three shallow bowls are set up. Place the hemp hearts in a pan. Whisk the egg, water, and vinegar together in the second bowl. The nutritional yeast, flax meal, garlic powder, and salt are combined in the fifth pan.
4. Grease the sheet pan gently.
5. Coat each tender lightly in the mixture of the flax meal, then dredge in the mix of the egg and finally cover it with the core of the hemp before putting it on the plate.
6. Cook fifteen minutes. Use a spatula to carefully turn each tender and cook for another 15 minutes.
7. Use a spatula to scrape up from the oven so that the breading does not stick to the sheet pan. Use your favorite sauce to eat.

**Macros** - Serving Size: 4 Calories: 558 Fat: 33.3g Carbohydrates: 7.4g Fiber: 7g Protein: 57.4g

**Prep time** 15 mins

## 170. CUCUMBER CAPRESE SALAD RECIPE

### Ingredients

- 1/2 cup cherry tomatoes
- One medium cucumber (roughly chopped)
- 1/2 cup mozzarella cheese (cut into 1

- One bunch basil (finely chopped)
- One small shallot (thinly sliced)
- Two tablespoons olive oil
- Two tablespoons balsamic vinegar
- One clove garlic (finely minced)
- 1/2 teaspoon salt
- 1/4 teaspoon pepper

## Instructions

1. Replace a medium-sized bowl of balsamic vinegar, olive oil, garlic, salt, and pepper. Play well with each other.
2. Add the bowl with cucumbers, onions, cheese, shallots, and basil. Toss gently until well covered.

**Macros** - Serving Size: 1/2 cup Calories: 112 Fat: 10g Carbohydrates: Net Carbs: 2g Protein: 4g

**Prep time** 5mins

# 171. GARLIC PARMESAN ZUCCHINI PASTA

## Ingredients

- Four medium zucchini (spiralized into noodles)
- Two tablespoons extra virgin olive oil
- Four cloves garlic
- 1/2 cup chopped tomatoes
- 1/2 cup shredded parmesan cheese
- 1 cup fresh basil leaves
- Two teaspoons lemon juice

## Instructions

1. Add olive oil, garlic, and red flakes of pepper in a skillet. When the oil begins to bubble with the garlic, add the zucchini's noodles. Throw the noodles and bake for 3-4 minutes. Turn the water off.
2. Incorporate onions, basil, lemon juice, parmesan cheese. Toss to dress up.
3. Serve with the option of grilled chicken, steak, or shrimp.
4. If required, garnish with additional parmesan cheese.

**Macros** - Serving Size: 1 cup Calories: 83 kcal Fat: 7g Carbohydrates: 5g Fiber: 2g Protein: 1g

**Prep time** 5 mins

# 172. CREAMED SPINACH

## Ingredients

- Four cloves garlic, sliced
- Two tablespoons ghee
- 1 pound raw baby spinach
- 1/2 teaspoon fine Himalayan salt
- Pinch of nutmeg
- 1/2 teaspoon black pepper
- 8 ounces lactose-free cream cheese

## Instructions

1. Place over medium heat a large skillet.
2. Add the garlic and ghee.
3. Bring in the spinach and cover the spinach quickly with a lid for 2-3 minutes.
4. Open the cover and stir well. Add salt, nutmeg, and pepper to taste.
5. Keep stirring until the spinach is dark green and release liquid once all the spinach is wilted.
6. Extract until the liquid evaporates, then blend until smooth and creamy in the cream cheese.
7. Serve immediately!

Macros - Calories: 162 Fat: 15g
Carbohydrates: 5g Fiber: 1g Protein: 3g

**Prep time** 5mins

**Servings** 4

## 173. JALAPEÑO PARMESAN CRISPS

### Ingredients

- One large jalapeno
- 1/4 tsp red pepper flakes
- 1/8 tsp pink salt
- 1/2 tsp dried oregano
- 1/2 cup grated parmesan, separated
- 1/4 cup finely shredded sharp cheddar

### Instructions

1. Preheat the oven to 425 degrees and use parchment paper to line a baking sheet.
2. Jalapeño slice thinly. Bake 5 minutes of sliced jalapeño.
3. Remove from the oven jalapeños, set aside, and allow cooling.
4. Whisk spices and parmesan together.
5. Pour 1 cup of spice and a mixture of parmesan into piles and flatten into small circles.
6. Place jalapeño sliced on top of the mixture of parmesan and spice. Sprinkle the cheddar cheese on top of the jalapeño.
7. Bake for eight minutes.
8. Enable the goodness to cool down and enjoy it!

Macros - Calories: 30 Fat: 2.3
Carbohydrates: 0.2 Protein: 2.5

**Prep time** 5 mins

**Servings** 10 to 12

## 174. CELERIAC OVEN FRIES

### Ingredients

- One large celeriac root
- 3 tbsp. coconut oil
- 2 tsp Everything Bagel Seasoning

### Instructions

1. Pre-heat 400F oven.
2. Cut off the celeriac's lower part, the twisted roots. Then peel the part of the round.
3. Cut and cut into slices. Soak the fries in water for 20 minutes with a little lemon.
4. Drain, rinse, and season with coconut oil.
5. Spread and bake for 30 minutes on a sheet pan, then turn off the oven and let them sit for another 10 minutes.
6. Open the oven; make a shake for the sheet pan.
7. Divvy your fries into four portions and prepare them for dipping with some homemade mayo!

### NOTES

Option for seasoning instead of Everything Bagel Seasoning: ½ tsp poppy seeds, ½ tsp sesame seeds, ½ tsp granulated garlic, ½ tsp salt)

Macros - Calories: 133 Fat: 9.8
Carbohydrates: 9 Protein: 1.5

**Prep time** 30mins

**Servings** 4

## 175. NO POTATO SALAD, AKA NO-TATO SALAD

## Ingredients

- One head Cauliflower
- ½ cup Keto-friendly mayo
- ¼ cup mustard
- Three hard-boiled eggs
- Four slices bacon, cooked
- Two stalks celery, chopped
- 2–3 tablespoons dill
- 2–3 tablespoons green onions, chopped
- One teaspoon of sea salt
- One teaspoon black pepper
- 1–2 tablespoons white wine vinegar
- One scoop Perfect Keto Unflavored Collagen

## Instructions

1. Combine and set aside the collagen in the mayo.
2. Remove all ingredients, including mayo and collagen, and use your hands to blend together.
3. Eat or hold chilled immediately until you are ready to serve.

**Macros** - Serving Size: 1Calories: 415Fat: 35.2gCarbohydrates: 9.8g (5.5g net)Fiber: 4.3gProtein: 25g

**Prep time** 20mins

**Servings** 4

## 176. CREAMY KETO SPINACH ARTICHOKE DIP

### Ingredient

- 1/2 cup of mozzarella cheese (shredded)
- 1/2 cup of parmesan (shredded)
- 1/4 cup of nutritional yeast

- 10 oz frozen spinach (thawed and drained)
- 12 oz artichoke hearts
- Two cloves garlic (finely chopped)
- 1/4 cup sour cream
- 1/2 cup cream cheese
- 1/4 cup mayonnaise
- 1/2 tsp salt
- 1/4 tsp pepper
- 1 tsp garlic powder

## Instructions

1. Preheat the oven to 375 ° C.
2. Add all ingredients in a large bowl. Mix well until everything is well mixed. Pour in a glass pie bowl or shallow baking dish. When necessary, finish with extra cheese.
3. Bake for about 20-25 minutes.

**Macros** - Serving Size: 1/2 cup Calories: 139Fat: 8g Carbohydrates: Net Carbs: 5g

**Prep time** 10 mins

**Servings** 2

## 177. SHEET PAN BRUSSELS SPROUTS WITH BACON

### Ingredients

- 16 oz bacon
- 16 oz raw brussels sprouts
- Salt and Pepper

### Instructions

1. Oven preheats to 400 degrees. Line baking sheet with paper on the parchment.
2. Half the sprouts of Brussels.
3. Cut bacon lengthwise into small pieces using kitchen shears.

4. In a prepared baking sheet, add brussels sprouts and bacon and season with salt and pepper.
5. Bake for 35-40 minutes until slightly browned brussels sprouts and crispy bacon.

**Macros** - Calories: 113 Fat: 6.9g Carbohydrates: 6.8g (3.9g net) Protein: 7.9g

**Servings** 6

**Prep time** 10 mins

# 178. KETO STIR FRY WITH CABBAGE NOODLES RECIPE

## Ingredients

- 1 pound of pastured chicken breast
- One head of green cabbage
- One clove of garlic (chopped)
- ½ white onion (diced)
- Two tablespoons of extra virgin olive oil

## Instructions

1. Heat a tablespoon of olive oil or wok over medium-high heat.
2. Attach the chopped garlic and cook to a minute for 30 seconds.
3. Cook 5-7 minutes or until translucent, add diced onion.
4. Add the remaining olive oil and chicken breast ground beef or chopped.
5. Stir fry until the chicken is crispy, or the ground beef is no longer pink for 3-5 minutes.
6. Chop the head of the cabbage into long strings like noodles while that's cooking.

7. Remove the amino of cabbage, bell pepper, and coconut — season with freshly grated ginger, sea salt, and black pepper.
8. Saute until the cabbage is soft but crispy for 3-5 minutes.
9. Finish with your favorite (optional) and seasoning sugar-free stir-fry sauce.
10. Serve on your own or over rice with cauliflower.

**Macros** - Serving Size: 4 Calories: 251 Fat: 14.8g Carbohydrates: 4.8g

**Prep time** 5mins

# 179. BAKED KETO SPAGHETTI SQUASH

## Ingredients

- One spaghetti squash
- 1 tbsp olive oil
- 1 tsp Himalayan sea salt
- 1 tsp pepper

## Instructions

1. Preheat the oven to 400 ° C.
2. Fill the sheet pan with parchment paper.
3. Split the spaghetti squash either way down the middle Drizzle the olive oil, salt, and pepper on the spaghetti squash Place the spaghetti squash on the plate and put it in the oven for 40 minutes.

**Macros** - Serving Size: 1 cup Calories: 31 Fat: 0.6g Carbohydrates: 7g (Net Carbs: 5.5g) Protein: 0.6g

**Prep time** 5min

# 180. GRILLED ASPARAGUS SALAD

## Ingredients

- One scoop Perfect Keto Micro Greens Powder
- One handful of Italian parsley
- Three tablespoons lemon juice
- One teaspoon lemon zest
- Four tablespoons extra virgin olive oil
- One tablespoon monk fruit or stevia
- ¾ teaspoon salt
- ½ teaspoon black pepper
- 1 lb asparagus

## Instructions

1. Heat a grill pan at medium-high heat or set the BBQ on fire.
2. With a tablespoon of olive oil, ¼ teaspoon salt, and a pinch of pepper, drizzle asparagus spears.
3. Grill asparagus up to slightly charred and tender for 5-6 minutes.
4. In the meantime, add Perfect keto greens to a high-speed blender by adding powder, parsley, lemon juice, lemon zest, olive oil, sweetener, and remaining salt and pepper. Mix all the way up to smooth. Change to taste the seasoning.
5. Cut asparagus into 1 "bits and use vinaigrette to drizzle. Toss to dress up. Serve cold, hot, or room temperature in a large bowl.

**Macros** - Serving Size: 1 serving Calories: 76 Fat: 7g Carbohydrates: 2g (1g net) Fiber: 1g Protein: 1g

**Servings** 4

**Prep time** 10mins

# KETO CHICKEN RECIPES

## 181. CHICKEN TINOLA

### Ingredient

- 2 lbs of chicken, 1 green papaya; sliced
- 4 cloves of garlic; 1 onion sliced
- 1 root ginger; sliced,
- 1/2 cup of malungay leaves
- Chicken broth, Fish sauce (Patis)

### Instructions

1. Sprinkle with garlic, onion, and ginger and add the chicken when the onion is translucent.
2. Spray with fish sauce until the chicken is light brown.
3. Simmer for some minutes or until mixture flavor is absorbed by the chicken.
4. Pour the broth of chicken and cook until the chicken is soft.
5. Add the papaya and drop the leaves when it is tender.
6. Serve and make the most of it!

**Macros** – 267 Cal 2g Carbs 14g Fat 25g Protein

**Prep time** – 10 mins

Servings – 2

## 182. CHICKEN-PORK ADOBO

### Ingredient

- 1-kilo pork; cut in 11/2" square thick
- 1 head garlic;

- 3 laurel leaves, 1/2 kilo of chicken; cut in serving pieces
- 8 tablespoons of soy sauce, 8 tablespoons of vinegar, 1 tablespoon of grounded black pepper
- 1 1/2 cup of rice water

### Instructions

1. In a saucepan, put all the ingredients together.
2. Boil until the chicken and pork are tender in medium heat.
3. Simmer until the consistency of the sauce is reached. When needed or according to the desired taste, season with soy sauce.
4. Serve warm!

**Macros** – 139 Cal 4g Carbs 9g Fat 10g Protein

**Prep time** – 5mins

**Servings** - 4

## 183. CHICKEN ADOBO IN COCONUT MILK

### Ingredients

- 1-kilo of chicken
- 4 cloves garlic; crushed, 1 small onion; minced, 1 potato; quartered (optional), 1 bell pepper; sliced (optional)
- 2 cups rice water, 1/2 cup vinegar, 1 cup thick coconut milk
- Fish sauce (patis), 2 bay leaves
- Salt to taste and Cooking oil.

### Instructions

1. Fry garlic and onion in oil in a saucepan.
2. In the brown season, add chicken with a small amount of fish sauce to taste.
3. Add water from the rice, vinegar, crushed garlic, leaves from the river.
4. Cook until the chicken is tender.
5. When there is little liquid left, add the milk of the coconut.
6. Simmer until the consistency of the sauce is achieved.
7. Season to taste with salt.
8. Remove and serve hot from the fire!

**Macros** – 720 Cal 23g Carbs 53g Fat 51g Protein

**Prep time** – 10 mins

**Servings** – 2

## 184. AFRITADA CHICKEN

### Ingredient

- 1/4 cup of cooking oil
- 1 large potato, cubed, 1 large carrot, cubed
- 2 lb. chicken, cut into serving pieces
- 3 pieces of bay leaves, 1 small onion, thinly sliced, 6 cloves garlic, minced
- 2 tablespoon fish sauce, 1/4 teaspoon ground black pepper
- 1 cup water, 1 cup tomato sauce (8 oz can), 1 red bell pepper, diced, 1/2 cup green peas, drained

### Optional Ingredient

- Salt to taste
- Pineapple
- Hotdog

### Instructions

1. Heat oil and pan-fry potatoes and carrots lightly browning on all sides in a pan over medium heat. Delete it and put it aside.
2. Sear the chicken in the same pan and brown lightly on each side. Delete it and put it aside.
3. Remove excess oil from the oven, leaving just approximately 2 tablespoons.
4. Saute the garlic and onion, respectively, until fragrant and translucent.
5. Return the seared chicken to the dish, then add the fish sauce and ground black pepper for 3 minutes, stirring occasionally.
6. Pour the water and tomato sauce into the bay leaves, then stir to mix the ingredients.
7. Cover, reduce HEAT TO LOW, and occasionally stir until the chicken is tender and thickens the sauce (about 20-25 minutes).
8. Attach potatoes and carrots to the dish, cover, and cook for 7 minutes or until tender.
9. Add bell peppers and green peas, mix and cook until done.
10. That's right. If required, season with salt and pepper.

**Macros** – 245 Cal 12g Carbs 9g Fat 28g Protein

**Prep time** – 10 mins

**Servings** - 1

## 185. SIMPLE SHEET PAN CHICKEN AND VEGGIES

### Ingredients

- 1 (0.7-oz.) packet Italian dressing mix
- 1-pound baby carrots, 1-pound baby Yukon Gold potatoes
- 2 tablespoons olive oil
- 4 to 6 bone-in, skin-on chicken thighs
- 8 ounces' French green beans
- 2 tablespoons butter (optional)

## Instructions

1. Power the oven up to 400 ° F. Reserve the Italian dressing blend for 1 tablespoon. Combine the carrots, onions, oil, and remaining dressing mixture together on an aluminum foil-lined baking sheet and arrange in a single layer.
2. Sprinkle the chicken with the reserved dressing mixture on top of the carrot and potato mixture.
3. Bake the chicken in a preheated oven until it is golden brown and insert a thermometer at 165 ° F, 35 to 40 minutes in the thickest section. Put the chicken on a plate.
4. Add green beans to the potato and carrot mixture. Add chicken back to the baking sheet with vegetables. Bake until the beans are crisp-tender at 400 ° F for about 7 minutes. Shake vegetables with butter if desired and serve with chicken.

**Macros** – 290 Cal 26g Carbs 14g Fat 18g Protein

**Prep time** – 5 mins

**Servings** – 4 to 6

## 186. CHICKEN INASAL

**Ingredients**

- 1-kilo chicken; breast and wings preferred, 4 stalks lemongrass; julienned
- Ground black pepper, 2 tablespoons 7-up or Sprite soda,
- 1 lemon; juice extracted, Skewers for grilling, Salt to taste, cooking oil
- 4 cloves garlic; crushed 1 lime; juice extracted,
- 2 tablespoons butter, 1/4 cup annatto seeds, Chili pepper flakes (optional)

## Instructions

1. Marinate chicken in salt, pepper, garlic, lemongrass, lime and lemon juice, and 7-up or Sprite soda overnight in a pan. Put it aside.
2. In cooking oil, fry annatto seeds. Let the annatto oil cool, crush, and drain in a pan. Put it aside.
3. By adding annatto oil, marinade, and butter, prepare a bashing mixture. Boil the pan for a few minutes and, if necessary, season with salt and MSG. Sometimes the Philippines have this tantra lang (estimate and approximate) cooking method. Experiment with your best combination, therefore.
4. Squeeze the chicken over the hot charcoal, brushing it once in a while with the mixture. Grill until finished.

**Macros** – 193 Cal 0g Carbs 8g Fat 26g Protein

**Prep time** – 10 mins

**Servings** - 6

## 187. FRIED MARINATED CHICKEN

## Ingredients

- 1-kilo chicken; cut into desired pieces
- 6 tablespoon fish sauce (patis)
- 1/4 tablespoon ground black pepper
- 1 lemon Cooking oil

## Instructions

1. In a fish sauce, pepper and lemon or Kalamaki, marinate chicken for 3 hours.
2. Deep fry until golden brown in hot cooking oil.
3. Serve warm!

**Macros** – 117 Cal 0g Carbs 5g Fat 16g Protein

**Prep time** – 5 mins

**Servings** - 4

## 188. SIMPLE SLOW COOKER WHOLE CHICKEN

### Ingredients

- 1 (4-lb.) whole chicken
- 2 teaspoons kosher salt
- 1 teaspoon black pepper

### Instructions

1. Remove chicken neck and giblets, discard or hold for further use, if necessary. Sprinkle with salt and pepper in and out of the chicken. In a slow cooker, place the chicken; cover and cook for 4 hours on LOW. Remove and discard the skin and bones of chicken and serve the chicken with accumulated juices or store meat and juices separately in airtight refrigerator containers for future use.

**Macros** – 159 Cal 1g Carbs 7g Fat 23g Protein

**Prep time** – 5 mins

**Servings** – 4 to 6

## 189. SIMPLE SHEET PAN CHICKEN AND VEGGIES

### Ingredients

- 1 (0.7-oz.) packet Italian dressing mix
- 1 pound baby carrots
- 1 pound baby Yukon Gold potatoes
- 2 tablespoons olive oil
- 4 to 6 bone-in, skin-on chicken thighs
- 8 ounces French green beans
- 2 tablespoons butter (optional)

### Instructions

1. Heat the oven up to 400 ° F. Reserve the Italian dressing blend for 1 tablespoon. Combine the carrots, onions, oil, and remaining dressing mixture together on an aluminum foil-lined baking sheet and arrange in a single layer.
2. Sprinkle chicken with reserved dressing mixture on top of the carrot and potato mixture.
3. Bake until the chicken is golden brown in a preheated oven and insert a thermometer in the thickest portion at 165 ° F, 35 to 40 minutes. Set on a tray with the chicken.
4. Add green beans to the potato and carrot mixture. Add the chicken back to the baking sheet on vegetables. Bake until the beans are crisp-tender at 400 ° F for about 7 minutes. If

required, shake buttered vegetables and serve with chicken.

**Macros** – 290 Cal 26g Carbs 14g Fat 18g Protein

**Prep time** – 15 mins

**Servings** - 6

## 190. PERFECT PAN-SEARED CHICKEN BREASTS

### Ingredients

- 4 (6-oz.) skinless, boneless chicken breast halves
- 1 teaspoon kosher salt
- 1/2 teaspoon freshly ground black pepper
- 1 tablespoon canola oil
- 1 teaspoon butter

### Instructions

1. With paper towels, thoroughly dry chicken; season with salt and pepper all over. Put the chicken on a tray in a rimmed baking sheet. Refrigerate for 30 minutes or overnight, uncovered. From the fridge lift, dry pat again.
2. Heat oil over medium-low in a 12-inch straight-sided sauté pan until it shimmers with heat. Put smooth side down the chicken. Cook for 9 minutes or until the light golden brown side is smooth, without turning, and chicken quickly releases from the pan. Apply butter; swirl to cover and raise the chicken so that the butter flows below. 1 minute or deep brown gold. Turn chicken; cook for 6 minutes or until 155 ° F is inserted into the breast

center by a thermometer. Remove the pan from heat; for 3 minutes, let the chicken stand in the bowl. Serve as soon as possible.

**Macros** – 231 Cal 1g Carbs 7g Fat 40g Protein

**Prep time** – 20 mins

**Servings** - 4

## 191. COCONUT CURRY CHICKEN

### Ingredient

- 1 1/3 4 boned, skinned chicken breast halves
- 3 tablespoons of butter, melted
- 1 cup of sweetened or unsweetened shredded dried coconut
- 2 teaspoons of curry powder
- Salt

### Instructions

1. Rinse your chicken and dry hand. Pour batter into a baking dish measuring 9-by 13-inch. Combine coconut and curry powder in a big, shallow bowl. Dip the chicken to cover in the butter and roll into the coconut. Layer pieces of chicken in the baking dish slightly apart. Pat any remaining mixture of coconut on top. Add salt to sprinkle.
2. Bake chicken in a 350 ° oven for 20 to 25 minutes, until it is no longer pink in the center of the thickest part.

**Macros** – 130 Cal 16g Carbs 5g Fat 6g Protein

**Prep time** – 10 mins

Servings – 4

## 192. BUFFALO CHICKEN PIZZA

### Ingredients

- Vegetable cooking spray
- 1/2 cup Buffalo-style hot sauce
- 1 (16-oz.) package prebaked Italian pizza crust
- 2 cups chopped deli-roasted whole chicken
- 1 cup (4 oz.) shredded provolone cheese
- 1/4 cup crumbled blue cheese

### Instructions

1. Coat the grill with the spray and put it on the grill. Preheat grill to 350 degrees (medium heat).
2. Spread the hot sauce over the crust, and the next 3 ingredients surface.
3. Place the crust on the cooking grate directly. Grill at 350 ° (medium heat) for 4 minutes, covered with the grill lid. Rotate one-quarter turn pizza and grill, covered with grill top, for 5 to 6 minutes or until heated thoroughly. Serve right away.

**Note**: We used Boboli pre-baked pizza crust for testing purposes only.

Buffalo Chicken Pizza Oven-Baked: Assemble pizza as guided and bake for pizza crust according to package directions.

**Macros** – 365 Cal 42g Carbs 11g Fat 24g Protein

**Prep time** – 10 mins

**Servings** – 5

## 193. CRISPY OVEN-FRIED DRUMSTICKS

### Ingredients

- 3 cups cornflake cereal, crushed
- 1/2 teaspoon salt, 1/4 to 1/2 tsp. ground red pepper, 1/4 teaspoon freshly ground black pepper
- 1/3 cup grated Parmesan cheese, 3/4 cup fat-free buttermilk
- 8 chicken drumsticks (about 2 lb.), skinned
- Vegetable cooking spray

### Instructions

1. In a big zip-top plastic freezer bag, mix the first 5 ingredients; seal and shake well to blend.
2. In a shallow bowl, add buttermilk. Dip 2 buttermilk drumsticks and put them in the bag. Seal and shake well, fully cover drumsticks. Place drumsticks coated with cooking spray on an aluminum foil-lined baking sheet. Repeat with the rest of the drumsticks. Sprinkle the remaining mixture of cornflake on the baking sheet uniformly over drumsticks. Coat lightly with spray for cooking.
3. Also, bake for 25 to 30 minutes at 425 ° or until the drumsticks are well browned and finished. Serve as soon as possible.

**Macros** – 171 Cal 15g Carbs 7g Fat 5g Protein

**Prep time** – 10 mins

**Servings** - 6

## 194. MESQUITE-SMOKED BEER CAN CHICKEN

### Ingredients

- 2 cups mesquite wood chips, 2 teaspoons chili powder
- 1 (4-pound) whole chicken
- 1 tablespoon olive oil 2 teaspoons brown sugar 1 teaspoon ground cumin 3/4 teaspoon kosher salt 1/2 teaspoon black pepper
- 1 (12-ounce) can beer

### Instructions

1. Thirty minutes soak wood chips in water; drain well.
2. Use both burners to preheat grill to medium-high heat. Turn off the left heater after preheating (leave the right heater on). Liberally pierce the bottom of an aluminum foil pan with a knife's tip. Place the container on the heating element on the grill side; add the chips of wood to the pan.
3. Remove from the chicken giblets and back, and discard. Beginning at the cavity of the chest, the skin is loosened from the breasts and drumsticks by inserting fingertips, pressing gently between skin and meat.
4. Combine oil in a bowl with the next 5 ingredients (by black pepper). Rub spice mixture on drumsticks and breasts under loosened skin; let stand for 20 minutes.
5. Dispose of 6 ounces of canale. Holding the chicken straight, facing the body cavity, pouring the beer into the hole. Place the chicken upright on the grill rack that covers the left burner and spread the legs to

form a tripod. Cover and grill for 1 1/2 hours or until 165 ° are inserted into thigh registers by a thermometer. Place the chicken on the cutting board and allow it to stand for 10 minutes.

**Macros** – 375 Cal 3g Carbs 17g Fat 51g Protein

**Prep time** – 40 mins

**Servings** - 4

## 195. SLOW COOKER CHICKEN CACCIATORE RECIPE

### INGREDIENTS

- Two cloves Garlic (minced)
- 1/2 large onion (diced)
- One large red bell pepper (diced)
- 1 14.5 oz of can diced tomatoes (drained)
- 1 tbsp fresh rosemary (chopped)
- 1 tbsp fresh thyme (chopped)
- Four medium chicken breasts
- 1 tsp Sea salt
- 1/4 tsp Black pepper
- One medium Bay leaf

### Instructions

1. Spice the chicken breasts with salt and pepper on both sides. Put in the slow cooker the chicken.
2. Stir the garlic, onion, bell peppers, diced tomatoes, rosemary, and thyme together in a medium bowl. Pour over the chicken the sauce uniformly.
3. Put a leaf in the center of the port.
4. Also, cover and cook for 3 to 4 hours or for 6 to 8 hours low.

5. Serve as soon as possible. If a thicker sauce is desired, remove the chicken and cook the sauce at low in the slow cooker for an additional hour.

**Macros** - Calories203 Fat3g Protein29g Total Carbs10g Net Carbs8g Fiber2g Sugar5g

**Servings** 4

**Prep time** 10 mins

## 196. CRISPY AIR FRYER CHICKEN WINGS RECIPE

### Ingredients

- 2 lb Chicken wings (flats and drumettes, either fresh or thawed from frozen)
- 1 tbsp Gluten-free baking powder
- 3/4 tsp Sea salt
- 1/4 tsp Black pepper

### Instructions

1. In a large bowl, combine baking powder, sea salt, and black pepper.
2. Grease 2 air-fryer oven shelves.
3. Place the wings on the greased trays or place in the basket just enough arms to be in one layer. (If you use a pan, you may need to cook in 2 lots.)
4. Place the basket or racks in the air fryer and bake at 250 degrees for 15 minutes.
5. Flip over the wings and turn the trays to the top and vice versa. Increase the temperature to 430 degrees (or your air fryer is going to be the highest). Air fried until chicken wings are finished and crispy for about 15 to 20 minutes.

**Macros** - Calories275 Fat19g Protein22g Total Carbs1g Net Carbs1g

**Servings** 4

**Prep time** 10 mins

## 197. LOW CARB CHICKEN ENCHILADAS RECIPE

### Ingredients

**Sauce**

- One recipe Gluten-free enchilada sauce (2 cups)
- Chicken
- 1 tbsp Avocado oil
- Four cloves Garlic (minced)
- 3 cups Shredded chicken (cooked)
- 1/4 cup Chicken broth
- 1/4 cup fresh cilantro (chopped)

**Assembly**

- One recipe Coconut tortillas (12 tortillas)
- 3/4 cup Colby jack cheese (shredded)
- 1/4 cup Green onions (chopped)

### Instructions

1. Heat oil over medium to high heat in a large saute pan. Attach the chopped garlic and cook until fragrant for about a minute.
2. Remove rice, 1 cup of enchilada sauce (half the total), chicken pasta, and coriander. Simmer for 5 minutes or so.
3. In the meantime, heat the oven to 375 degrees F. Grease a baking dish of 9x13.
4. Cut into the middle of each tortilla around 1/4 cup chicken mixture. In

the baking dish, roll up and place the seam side down.

5. Pour over the enchiladas the remaining 1 cup of enchilada sauce. Sprinkle with cheese that is shredded.

6. Bake until the enchiladas are hot and the cheese melts for about 10 to 12 minutes. Sprinkle with serving green onions.

**Macros** - Calories349 Fat19g Protein31g Total Carbs17g Net Carbs9g Fiber8g Sugar3g

**Servings** 6

**Prep time** 20 mins

## 198. GREEK CHICKEN MEAL PREP BOWLS RECIPE

### Ingredient

- 1 lb of Chicken breast
- 1 1/2 tsp of Sea salt
- 3 tbsp of Olive oil
- 1 tbsp of Balsamic vinegar (optional)
- 1/2 tsp of Black pepper (divided)
- 10 oz of Zucchini (sliced into thin half-moons, 1/4 inch thick, ~2.5 cups)
- 1/2 lb of Grape tomatoes
- 1/2 large onion, 1/4 cup of Feta cheese,
- 1/2 tbsp of dried dill
- 1/2 tbsp of Dried parsley
- 1 tsp of dried oregano
- 1 tsp of Garlic powder

### Instructions

1. Preheat the oven to 400 F. Line an extra-large foil-and-grease sheet pan well.

2. Fill with water a large bowl. Add salt for two cubic meters and stir to dissolve. Add the chicken and set aside for 10 to 20 minutes to brine.

3. In the meantime, cut veggies, such as zucchini, grape tomatoes, and onions.

4. Stir the dried dill, parsley, oregano, and garlic powder in a small bowl.

5. Stick together but not touching when the chicken is cooked, brin, pat dry, and put in one region of the baking sheet.

6. Use a spoonful of olive oil to wash both sides of the chicken. To season on both sides of the chicken, use 3/4 tsp sea salt and 1/4 tsp black pepper. Sprinkle with the herb mixture on both sides, using half of it.

7. Meanwhile, toss the chopped vegetables and the other two tablespoons of olive oil in a large bowl. Add the remaining 3/4 tsp of sea salt, 1/4 tsp of black pepper, and the rest of the blend of herbs. Toss well for mixing. Set the veggies on the baking sheet in a single layer to make sure they're not over the chicken.

8. Roast in the oven for about 20 minutes the chicken and vegetables until the vegetables are soft and the chicken is cooked through. Remove from the oven and allow the pan to rest for five minutes.

9. Slice the chicken and move the containers to the meal preparation. Fill with vegetables the rest. Sprinkle with feta cheese if you're not milk-free.

**Macros** Calories287 Fat15g Protein28g Total Carbs7g Net Carbs6g Fiber1g Sugar4gCalories287

**Servings** 4

**Prep time** 20mins

## 199. CREAMY GARLIC CHICKEN THIGHS RECIPE

### Ingredient

- 1 1/3 lb of boneless skinless chicken thighs
- 1/2 tsp of Sea salt
- 1/4 tsp of smoked paprika
- 1/8 tsp of Black pepper
- 2 tbsp of butter (divided)
- 1/2 head Garlic
- 1/2 cup of chicken bone broth
- 1/2 cup of white cooking wine
- 1/4 cup of Heavy cream
- 1 medium Bay leaf

### Instructions

1. Season the chicken with salt, pepper, and smoked paprika on both sides.
2. Heat 1 tablespoon (30 grams) of butter over medium-high heat in a large skillet or saute pan. Add the chicken and sear until browned and cooked through for 5 to 7 minutes per side, without moving.
3. Take the chicken from the saucepan and cover it with foil.
4. Add the remaining spoonful of butter (30 grams) to the pan. Add the garlic that has been cut. Saute until the garlic is fragrant and begin to brown for 2-3 minutes, stirring frequently.

5. Remove the bread and wine to the saucepan. Use a wooden spoon to scrape any brown bits (this is called de-glazing) from the bottom.
6. Put the leaf of the bay in the pan and plunge. Bring the fluid to a gentle boil, then raise heat and cook for 8-12 minutes until half of the volume is depleted.
7. Add the cream to the casserole. Heat (do not boil) for just a few minutes.
8. Remove the leaf from the bay and return the chicken to the pan. Spoon the chicken with the sauce.

**Macros** -
Calories297Fat17gProtein30gTotal Carbs1gNet Carbs1g

**Servings** - 4

**Prep time** - 5 mins

## 200. KETO LOW CARB GLUTEN-FREE CHICKEN AND DUMPLINGS RECIPE

### Ingredients

- 1 tbsp Olive oil
- 1/2 large Onion
- 1 large Carrot
- 1 stalk Celery
- 2 tsp Italian seasoning
- 1 1/2 lb Chicken breast
- 8 cups Chicken broth
- 2 medium Dried bay leaves
- 1/2 recipe Fathead bagel dough

### Instructions

1. Add olive oil, potatoes, onions, and celery. Saute until tender for about 10 minutes.

2. Attach the seasoning in Italy. Saute to a fragrant finish.

3. Add the chicken, chicken broth, and leaves of the bay (raw). The lid is closed and locked. Set for 6 minutes for manual high pressure. Use the quick release to release pressure when the soup is cooked.

4. While, use the same instructions and quantities as the fathead bagels recipe to make fathead bread, except to break the method in half. (Either enter "3" in the bagel serving box, OR make the whole dough recipe, but use only half of it for keto chicken and dumplings.)

5. If the dough is soft, refrigerate until firm for approximately 20 minutes.

6. Place the fathead dough between two parchment paper pieces. Roll out, about 1/4 in (.5 cm) thick, to a rectangle. Cut into strips with a width of about 2 in (5 cm)x 1/2 in (1 cm).

7. Remove the lid when the soup is done, and pressure is released. Remove leaves from the harbor.

8. Cut the chicken and cut into pieces (or shreds) of bite-size. Go back to the Instant Pot.

9. Set the Saute mode to the Instant Pot again. Add the hits. Disable for approximately 3 minutes before cooking.

**Macros** - Calories273 Fat14g Protein28g

Total Carbs5g Net Carbs4g Fiber1g

**Servings** - 8

**Prep time** - 20 mins

# 2 WEEK MEAL PLAN

## WEEK 1

### DAY 1

**BREAKFAST** (makes three servings)

**MINI CRUSTLESS QUICHES**

**Ingredients**

- 14 large eggs.
- Three plum of tomatoes, diced ⅔ cup mozzarella cheese, shredded.
- ⅓ cup pepper jack cheese, shredded, ⅓ cup sliced pickled jalapenos.
- ⅓ cup sweet onion, diced.
- ⅓ cup heavy cream, ⅔ cup soppressata salami, diced.

**Instructions**

1. Preheat the oven to 325 ° F and grate a muffin tin of 15"x 11."
2. In a mixing bowl, combine all the ingredients, season with salt and pepper, and whisk well.
3. Divide the quiche batter equally into the muffin tin and bake for about 25 minutes.
4. Store in the refrigerator and heat when you are ready to eat.
5. Four Mini Crustless Quiches are focused on food. The food is about twelve.

**Macros** Calories: 382, 28F, 22P, 5.3C

**LUNCH**

**HAM & CHEDDAR WRAPS**

**Ingredients**

- One low carb wrap.
- 2 tbsp mayonnaise.
- 2 oz. Cheddar, shredded.
- 2 oz. Deli ham.
- Pickles or jalapenos to taste.
- Salt, pepper.

**Instructions**

1. Spread the mayonnaise on a low carb cover.
2. 2. Add the shredded cheese and slices of ham.
3. 3. If you're looking for something fresh and juicy, add some pickles or jalapenos.
4. 4. Cover it tightly and cut it to match or enjoy your lunch bag instantly!

**Macros** - Calories: 600, 44F, 27P, 8C

**DINNER**

**CHICKEN & MUSHROOMS**

**Ingredients**

- 6 oz. Chicken breast, 8 oz. white mushrooms.
- 2 tbsp butter.
- ¼ cup of water, ¼ cup heavy cream
- 1 tsp fresh lemon juice.
- Salt, pepper, one handful of spinach

**Instructions**

1. Cook the chicken on a saucepan until it is cooked almost all the way. Then let it

rest on a plate during the preparation of the sauce.

2.   Cook the mushrooms on the same pan in butter until they crisp and shrink.

3.   Add water, juice of lemon, and heavy cream and cook until thickened.

4.   Season with salt and pepper to bring the chicken back in to cook the rest of the way. Serve with a side of spinach.

**Macros** - Calories: 640, 51F, 46P, 5C

# DAY 2

## BREAKFAST

## MINI CRUSTLESS QUICHES

### Ingredients

- 14 large eggs
- three plum of tomatoes, diced
- ⅔ cup of mozzarella cheese, shredded, ⅓ cup of pepper jack cheese, shredded, ⅓ cup sweet onion, diced, ⅓ cup sliced pickled jalapenos
- ⅔ cup soppressata salami, diced
- ⅓ cup heavy cream

### Instructions

1.   Preheat the oven to 325 ° F and grate a muffin tin of 15"x 11."
2.   In a mixing bowl, combine all the ingredients, season with salt and pepper, and whisk well.
3.   Divide the quiche batter equally into the muffin tin and bake for about 25 minutes.

4.   Store in the refrigerator and heat when you are ready to eat.
5.   Nutrition is based on 4 Mini Quiches

**Macros** - Calories: 382, 28F, 22P, 5.3C

## LUNCH

## BLT AVOCADO WRAPS

### Ingredients

- Three lettuce leaves
- 3 tbsp mayonnaise
- Six strips bacon, cooked
- ½ Roma tomato, sliced, ½ avocado, sliced
- Salt and pepper

### Instructions

1.   Gently flatten the leaves of lettuce and spread on each one a tablespoon of mayo.
2.   Place two strips of bacon on each branch, then the sliced tomato and avocado.
3.   Salt and pepper season.
4.   Tightly wrap each one and enjoy it!

**Macros** - Calories: 640, 56F, 18P, 6C

## DINNER

## LOW CARB CHICKEN QUESADILLA

### Ingredients

- One low carb wrap
- 3 oz. Pepper jack cheese, shredded, 2.5 oz. chicken breast, grilled, shredded
- ½ avocado, sliced thin
- 1 tsp chopped jalapeño
- ¼ tsp salt

## Instruction

1. Put the wrap on a frying pan wide enough to make it as flat as possible to place the wrap on medium heat.
2. Flip the cover over after 2 minutes and start laying out the pepper jack. Don't get to the corners too close.
3. Add half of the wrap to the chicken breast, avocado, and jalapeño.
4. Use a spatula to fold the cover and press down to flatten. This will mean that the quesadilla together will be melted cheese glues.
5. 5. Remove the casserole and cut it into thirds. Treat yourself to salsa and sour cream!

**Macros** - Calories: 654, 43F, 52P, 7C

# DAY 3

## BREAKFAST

## MINI CRUSTLESS QUICHES

### Ingredients

- 14 large eggs, ⅓ cup sweet onion, diced,
- three plum of tomatoes, diced ⅔ cup mozzarella cheese, shredded,
- ⅓ cup pepper jack cheese, shredded
- ⅓ cup sliced pickled jalapenos, ⅓ cup heavy cream
- ⅔ cup soppressata salami, diced

### Instructions

1. Preheat the oven to 325 ° F and grate a muffin tin of 15"x 11."

2. In a mixing bowl, add all the ingredients, season with salt and pepper, and whisk well.
3. Divide the quiche batter equally into the muffin tin and bake for about 25 minutes.
4. Put in the fridge and steam when you are ready to eat.
5. Nutrition is based on 4 Mini Quiches

**Macros** - Calories: 382, 28F, 22P, 5.3C

## LUNCH

## EASY COBB SALAD

### Ingredients

- One large hard-boiled egg
- 4 oz. chicken breast
- 1 cup spinach
- two strips of bacon, ¼ avocado.
- 1 tbsp olive oil, ½ tsp white vinegar

### Instructions

1. Cook the egg for 10 minutes, bring a pot of water to boil. Heat it in cold water once it is cooked and chop it.
2. Cook the chicken breast and bacon on a frying pan to produce the desired crispiness.
3. Spinach leaves roughly chop or rip and add to the bacon, chicken, and chopped egg.
4. Drop an avocado in half and mix it to break it down.
5. Use a low carb Bleu cheese dressing and dress with olive oil and vinegar.

**Macros** - Calories: 600, 48F, 43P, 2C

## DINNER (MAKES FOUR SERVINGS)

## CHEDDAR CHICKEN & BROCCOLI CASSEROLE

### Ingredients

- 20 oz. chicken breast, shredded
- 2 cups broccoli florets (we used frozen), 1 cup cheddar cheese, shredded
- 2 tbsp olive oil, 1 tsp oregano
- ½ cup sour cream, ½ cup heavy cream
- 1 oz. pork rinds, crushed

### Instructions

1. Preheat to 450 ° F in the oven.
2. Combine chicken, broccoli flowers, olive oil, and sour cream in a large mixing bowl. Mix well to blend.
3. Put the mixture in a greased 8x11 "baking dish and press into a sheet.
4. Drizzle the whole segment of the heavy cream. Using salt, pepper, and oregano to season.
5. Apply the cheddar cheese to the bottom, and for a crispy casserole, top apply the crushed pork rinds over the milk.
6. Bake for 20-25 minutes or so.
7. Nutrition is the casserole per ¼.

**Macros** - Calories: 548, 42F, 44P, 4C

## DAY 4

## BREAKFAST (MAKES THREE SERVINGS)

## CHOCOLATE PEANUT BUTTER MUFFINS

### Ingredient

- 1 tsp baking powder
- One pinch salt
- ⅓ cup peanut butter, ⅓ cup almond milk
- Two large eggs, ½ cup erythritol
- ½ cup SF chocolate chips, 1 cup almond flour

### Instructions

1. Combine and stir in a large mixing bowl all the dry ingredients (except chocolate chips).
2. Remove and mix peanut butter and almond milk.
3. Add 1 egg at a time, each fully incorporating.
4. Fold in the chips of the SF chocolate.
5. Sprinkle a pan of muffin and add the butter. Bake for like 15 minutes at 350 ° F. This recipe produces six muffins per serving, two muffins.
6. Nutrition is for 2 peanut butter muffins with chocolate.

**Macros** - Calories: 530, 41F, 15P, 4.5C

## LUNCH

## TUNA AVOCADO SALAD

### Ingredient

- 4 oz. canned tuna
- ½ stalk celery, diced,

- 2 tbsp of mayonnaise, 1 tsp of mustard, ½ tsp fresh lemon juice
- Salt, pepper, ½ avocado
- One hard-boiled egg, peeled, chopped

## Instructions

1. Combine the salmon, celery, and avocado.
2. Remove mayo, vinegar, lemon juice, and spices.
3. Add the egg to the tuna salad.
4. Blend together until all the ingredients are well mixed.

**Macros** - Calories: 508, 34F, 31P, 5C

## DINNER

## CHEDDAR CHICKEN & BROCCOLI CASSEROLE

## Ingredient

- 20 oz. of chicken breast, shredded
- 2 cups of broccoli florets (we used frozen), 2 tbsp olive oil
- ½ cup sour cream, 0½ cup heavy cream
- Salt, pepper
- 1 tsp of oregano, 1 cup of cheddar cheese, shredded, 1 oz. of pork rinds, crushed

## Instructions

1. Preheat to 450 ° F in the oven.
2. Combine chicken, broccoli, olive oil, and sour cream in a large mixing bowl. Mix well to combine.
3. Put the mixture in a greased 8x11 "baking dish and press into a layer.
4. Drizzle the whole surface of heavy cream. Salt, pepper, and oregano season.

5. Add the cheddar cheese, and for a crispy casserole, top add the crushed pork rinds over the cheese.
6. Bake for 20-25 minutes or so.
7. Nutrition is the casserole per ¼.

**Macros** - Calories: 548, 42F, 44P, 4C

## DAY 5

## BREAKFAST

## CHOCOLATE PEANUT BUTTER MUFFINS

## Ingredient

- 1 cup of almond flour, ½ cup erythritol, 1 tsp baking powder
- One pinch salt
- ⅓ cup peanut butter, ⅓ cup almond milk
- large eggs
- ½ cup SF chocolate chips

## Instructions

1. Combine and stir in a large mixing bowl all the dry ingredients (except chocolate chips).
2. Remove and mix peanut butter and almond milk.
3. Add 1 egg at a time, each entirely incorporated.
4. Fold in the chips of SF chocolate.
5. Sprinkle a tin of muffin and add the batter. Bake at 350 ° F for 15 minutes.
6. This recipe produces six muffins per serving, two muffins.
7. Nutrition is for 2 peanut butter muffins of chocolate.

**Macros** - Calories: 530, 41F, 15P, 4.5C

## LUNCH

## CHEDDAR CHICKEN & BROCCOLI CASSEROLE

### Ingredient

- 20 oz. of chicken breast, shredded
- 2 cups of broccoli florets (we used frozen), 2 tbsp olive oil, ½ cup sour cream, ½ cup heavy cream
- Salt, pepper
- 1 tsp of oregano, 1 cup of cheddar cheese, shredded
- 1 oz. of pork rinds, crushed

### Instructions

1. Preheat to 450 ° F in the oven.
2. Combine chicken, broccoli, olive oil, and sour cream in a large mixing bowl. Mix well to combine.
3. Place the mixture in a greased 8x11 "baking dish and press into a layer.
4. Drizzle the whole surface of heavy cream. Use salt, pepper, and oregano to season.
5. Add the cheddar cheese and add the crushed pork rinds on top of the cheese for a crispy casserole.
6. Bake for 20-25 minutes or so.
7. Nutrition is the casserole per ¼.

**Macros** - Calories: 548, 42F, 44P, 4C

## DINNER

## SHRIMP & MUSHROOM ZOODLES

### Ingredients

- 1 tbsp olive oil
- 8 oz. white mushrooms, sliced
- 1 tbsp butter

- 6 oz. large shrimp, peeled
- One large zucchini
- ¼ cup marinara sauce
- Salt, pepper
- 2 tbsp Parmesan cheese

### Instruction

1. Heat the olive oil in a pan.
2. Fry the mushrooms until the oil have been soaked.
3. Add butter and cook the mushrooms until golden.
4. Add the shrimp and cook on each side for about 4 minutes.
5. While the shrimp are cooking, use a spiralizer to create the zoodles.
6. 6. Throw the zoodles in for 2 minutes after the shrimps are cooked and pink.
7. Then add salt and pepper to the marinara sauce and season.
8. Love a Parmesan sprinkle!

**Macros** - Calories: 500, 32F, 44P, 7.5C

# DAY 6

## BREAKFAST

## CHOCOLATE PEANUT BUTTER MUFFINS

### Ingredients

- 1 cup almond flour, ½ cup erythritol
- 1 tsp baking powder, ½ cup SF chocolate chips
- One pinch salt
- ⅓ cup peanut butter, ⅓ cup almond milk
- Two large eggs

### Instructions

1. Combine and stir in a large mixing bowl all the dry ingredients (except chocolate chips).
2. Add and combine peanut butter and almond milk.
3. Add 1 egg at a time, each fully incorporating.
4. Fold in the chips of SF chocolate.
5. Sprinkle a tin of muffin and add the butter. Bake for 15 minutes at 350 ° F.
6. Nutrition is for 2 peanut butter muffins of chocolate.

**Macros** - Calories: 530, 41F, 15P, 4.5C

## LUNCH

## CHEDDAR CHICKEN & BROCCOLI CASSEROLE

### Ingredient

- 20 oz. of chicken breast, shredded
- 2 cups of broccoli florets (we used frozen)
- 2 tbsp olive oil, ½ cup sour cream, ½ cup heavy cream
- Salt, pepper
- 1 tsp oregano, 1 cup cheddar cheese, shredded, 1 oz. pork rinds, crushed

### Instructions

1. Preheat to 450 ° F in the oven.
2. Combine chicken, broccoli, olive oil, and sour cream in a large mixing bowl. Mix well to combine.
3. Place the mixture in a greased 8x11 "baking dish and press into a sheet.
4. Drizzle the whole layer of heavy cream. Salt, pepper, and oregano season.
5. Add the cheddar cheese and add the crushed pork rinds over the cheese to a crispy casserole, lid.
6. Bake for 20-25 minutes or so.
7. Nutrition is the casserole per ¼.

**Macros** - Calories: 548, 42F, 44P, 4C

## DINNER

## SRIRACHA LIME FLANK STEAK

### Ingredients

- 7 oz. asparagus
- 8 oz. flank steak
- Salt, pepper, Sriracha Lime Sauce:
- ½ lime, 1 tbsp sriracha, ½ tsp vinegar
- Salt, pepper, 1 tbsp olive oil

### Instructions

1. Trim the ends off the asparagus and fry them for about 10 minutes on medium heat, sometimes tossing.
2. Dress the steak with salt and pepper in a liberal way. Broil for medium-rare 5 minutes on each side. For medium and well done, add 1 minute on each side and 2 minutes.
3. Cover the steak and allow 5 minutes to rest. In the meantime, in a pan, squeeze fresh lime and mix with sriracha, vinegar, salt, and pepper. Slowly pour in olive oil while whisking these together to create an emulsion and thicken the sauce.
4. Slice thin steak and serve with asparagus and sauce. Enjoy!

**Macros** - Calories: 560, 34F, 52P, 8C

# DAY 7

## BREAKFAST

## CREAMY SCRAMBLED EGGS

### Ingredients

- Four large eggs
- 2 tbsp butter
- Four strips bacon
- 2 tbsp sour cream
- ½ tsp salt, ¼ tsp black pepper
- One stalk green onion

### Instructions

1. Crack eggs and add medium-high heat butter to a pan. With a silicone spatula, stir continuously.

2. 2. Let some strips of bacon cook in another pot while stirring the eggs (or baking them).
3. Alternate in 30-second intervals to mix the eggs on the heat and off the water. Turn off the heat when they're nearly done. The eggs will continue to cook a bit more out of the pan's residual heat.
4. Season with salt and pepper and add a tablespoon of sour cream.
5. Garnish and enjoy with chopped green onion!
6.

**Macros** - Calories: 710, 57F, 37P, 2.5C

## LUNCH (MAKES THREE SERVINGS)

## CHICKEN ZOODLE SOUP

### Ingredients

- 2 tbsp olive oil, ½ white onion, chopped
- One medium carrot, chopped
- One stalk celery, chopped
- 1 tbsp dried oregano
- 1-quart chicken broth
- 8 oz. boneless, skinless chicken thighs
- One large zucchini
- ¼ cup sour cream

### Instructions

1. 1. Heat olive oil in a medium heat soup pot and cook onion until translucent.
2. Season with salt, pepper, and oregano, add carrots and celery. Cook until slightly softened.
3. Add the broth of chicken and bring to a boil the mixture. Then reduce

the heat to an oven, remove the chicken and cook for 30 minutes.

4. Remove and shred the thighs of the chicken. Cook for another 15 minutes.
5. In the last 2 or 3 minutes of cooking, spiral the zucchini into thin noodles and add them to the soup. Enjoy the sour cream soup!
6. Nutrition is one-third of the recipe

**Macros** - Calories: 370, 26F, 23P, 8C

Stretch, fold, and enjoy with some mayo!

**Macros** - Calories: 640, 59F, 24P, 1C

## DINNER

## BUNLESS BUTTER BURGER

### Ingredient

- 4 oz. of ground beef
- Salt, pepper
- 1 tsp paprika, 1 tbsp butter, 1 tbsp olive oil
- One large leaf of lettuce, One slice cheese
- 1 tsp mayonnaise

### Instructions

1. Add salt, pepper, and paprika to the ground beef and mix well with your hands.
2. Make two flat patties and put the butter in one of the patties in the center.
3. Place the second patty over the buttered patty and press and seal the sides until the two patties are mixed.
4. Cook the patty on a saucepan with high heat olive oil on each side for 4 minutes.
5. Place the patty on a lettuce leaf once it's finished and add a slice of cheese.

# WEEK 2

## DAY 1

### BREAKFAST

### CREAMY COFFEE SHAKE

### Ingredients

- 1 cup brewed coffee
- ¼ cup heavy cream
- 1 tbsp coconut oil
- One scoop vanilla protein powder (about 30 grams)

### Instructions

1. Add a blender or nutribullet to the brewed coffee.
2. Add the heavy cream, coconut oil, and protein powder to it. A low carb like Isopure or NowFoods is recommended.
3. Blend for about 20 seconds at the tip.
4. Be careful to open the blender because a lot of steam may have been created by the hot coffee. 5. Enjoy the warm weather!

**Macros** - Calories: 425, 38F, 25P, 1C

### LUNCH

### CHICKEN ZOODLE SOUP

### Ingredients

- 2 tbsp olive oil, ½ white onion, chopped
- One medium carrot, chopped
- One stalk celery, chopped • 1 tbsp dried oregano

- 1-quart chicken broth, 8 oz. boneless, skinless chicken thighs
- One large zucchini • ¼ cup sour cream

### Instructions

1. Heat olive oil in a soup pot and cook onion until it becomes translucent.
2. Add carrots and celery and add salt, pepper, and oregano to the season. Cook until slightly softened.
3. Add the broth of chicken and bring to a boil the mixture. Then reduce the heat to an oven, remove the chicken and cook for 30 minutes.
4. Cut and cut the thighs of the chicken. Cook for another 15 minutes.
5. In the last 2 or 3 minutes of cooking, spiralize the zucchini into thin noodles and add them to the soup. Love the sour cream soup!
6. Nutrition is one-third of the recipe.

**Macros** - Calories: 370, 26F, 23P, 8C

### DINNER

### LOW CARB CHICKEN QUESADILLA

### Ingredients

- One low carb wrap
- 3 oz. Pepper jack cheese, shredded, 2.5 oz. chicken breast, grilled, shredded
- ½ avocado, sliced thin
- 1 tsp chopped jalapeño
- ¼ tsp salt

### Instructions

1. Place the wrap on a frying pan wide enough to allow the wrap to be placed on medium heat as flat as possible.

2. After 2 minutes, turn the wrap over and continue to lay the pepper jack. Do not get too close to the corners. Add half of the wrap to the chicken breast, avocado, and jalapeño.
3. With a spatula, turn the cover over and press down to flatten. This will mean that the quesadilla is filled with the melted cheese glues.
4. Replace the pan and cut it into thirds. Treat yourself to salsa and sour cream!

**Macros** - Calories: 654, 43F, 52P, 7C

## DAY 2

### BREAKFAST

### AVOCADO BOAT, SAUSAGE & ASPARAGUS

### Ingredients

- 60g sausage
- 1-2 asparagus
- 1 tsp olive oil
- 1/2 avocado 70g tuna
- 1/4 cup wilted spinach (50g fresh)
- 1 tbsp mayo pinch salt & pepper

### Instructions

1. Heat the olive oil and fry the sausages and asparagus until it is cooked. Move to a plate.
2. Scoop the avocado inside and put it in a bowl with the salmon, wild spinach, mayo, and salt & pepper. Stuff the shell of the avocado and place it on the table.

**Macros** - 537 calories 42.29g fat 11.2g carbs 8.3g fiber 1.3g sugar 30.78g protein

### LUNCH

### ROSEMARY SHRIMPS & RADISHES

### Ingredients

- Five radishes (85g)
- Ten shrimps (100g)
- Three broccoli florets (60g)
- 1 tbsp rosemary
- 1 tbsp olive oil
- 1/2 tsp salt, pepper

### Instructions

1. In a pan, put a little water to boil and add the broccoli. Cook until you are ready.
2. Heat the oil in a skillet and add the radishes on one side and the shrimps on the other side. Sprinkle the salt, pepper, and rosemary with a few minutes of cooking. Soft and crunchy should be the radishes, and orange should be the shrimps.
3. Put it all on a plate to enjoy.

# DAY 3

## BREAKFAST

### EGGS, BACON & TOMATO SALAD

#### Ingredients

- Three slices of bacon
- Two eggs 1/4 red pepper
- 1/4 zucchini (40g), pinch salt & pepper
- Three slices tomato
- One basil leaf, 1 tsp olive oil, One garlic clove, 1/2 tsp vinegar sprinkle salt & pepper

#### Instructions

1. Slice the zucchini and the red pepper.
2. Fry the bacon until it is crispy in a small non-stick frying pan. Put on a plate, the bacon. In the bacon fat, fry the peppers and zucchini until tender, open the eggs, and scramble until cooked. Sprinkle with salt and pepper. Place the bacon on the plate.
3. Mince the clove of garlic and leaf of basil. Add the olive oil, basil, garlic, vinegar, salt, and pepper in a small bowl. Add the slices of tomato to the plate and pour over the dressing.

**Macros** 541 calories 39.81g fat 8.12g carbs 1.8g fiber 4.42g sugar 36.3g protein

## LUNCH

### CHICKEN BROCHETTES & EASY SALAD

#### Ingredients

- Three chicken brochettes
- Five lettuce leaves
- 1/4 red pepper
- One slice tomato
- 1 tbp sesame dressing

#### Instructions

1. Rip the lettuce in pieces of bite-size. Slice the tomato and red pepper. Remove the dressing of sesame and cover it well.
2. Add the brochettes and the salad to a bowl.

**Macros** - 400 calories 26.29g fat 13.28g carbs 4.2g fiber 5.89g sugar 27.92g protein

## DINNER

### LETTUCE-WRAPPED BURGER

#### Ingredients

- 70g ground beef
- Two slices of bacon (50g) (18g cooked)
- One large lettuce leaf
- 1 cup fresh baby spinach
- One slice tomato 1 tbsp mayo

#### Instructions

1. 1. Fry the bacon in a pan until it's crispy. With the ground beef, form a hamburger patty and fry in the remaining bacon grease. Cook until cooked on both sides.
2. In the skillet, add the spinach to the remaining grease and cook until wilted.
3. In a large leaf of lettuce, add the mayo, tomato, spinach, patty and bacon, fold and make a burger!

**Macros** - 358 calories 31.24g fat 2.76g carbs 1.3g fiber 1.19g sugar 16g protein

# DAY 4

## BREAKFAST

## AVOCADO BOAT, SAUSAGES & SCRAMBLED EGGS

### Ingredients

- 60g sausage, Two mushrooms
- Two eggs,
- 1/4 spinach, 1 tbsp olive oil pinch salt & pepper
- 1/2 avocado, 70g of tuna can
- 1 tbsp of mayo, 1 tsp sliced of green onion

### Instructions

1. Slice the mushrooms.
2. Heat the oil and cook the sausages in a small non-stick frying pan. Add them to a plate once cooked. Fry the fresh spinach and mushrooms until soft and add the eggs. Scramble to bake, sprinkle with salt and pepper, and add to the bowl.
3. Excavate the inside of the avocado and combine in a small bowl with the green onions, salmon, mayo, and pepper. Refill the bowl ingredients with the avocado shell and place them on the table.

**Macros** - 792 calories 64.82g fat 11.23g carbs 7.5g fiber 2.19g sugar 42.93g protein

## LUNCH

## CHICKEN BROCHETTES & SESAME SALAD

### Ingredients

- Three chicken & veggie brochettes
- three lettuce leaves
- one tomato slice
- 1/4 avocado
- 1 tbsp sesame dressing

### Instructions

1. Rip the lettuce in pieces of bite-size. Slice the avocado out and cube it, slice in a few parts the tomato slice. Add the dressing of sesame and cover it well.
2. Remove the brochettes and the salad to a bowl.

**Macros** - 468 calories 33.53g fat 14.89g carbs 6.7g fiber 4.44g sugar 28.35g protein

## DINNER

## ARUGULA SALAD WITH BASIL VINAIGRETTE

### Ingredients

- 40g arugula
- 1/2 tomato, 5-6 slices cucumber
- two slices prosciutto (20g)
- Three broccoli florets (50g)
- 1 serving Basil Vinaigrette

### Instructions

1. In a pot, place some water and add the broccoli. Cook under cold water until smooth and crisp.
2. Mix all the ingredients in a bowl and serve them on a plate!

**Macros** - 269 calories 22.54g fat 10.46g carbs 2.9g fiber 3.96g sugar 9.09g protein

# DAY 5

## BREAKFAST

## FLUFFY OMELETTE & VEGGIES

### Ingredients

- 1/2 red pepper
- 30g swiss chard
- Three mushrooms
- 1 tsp olive oil pinch salt, pepper, garlic powder
- Two eggs 1 tsp olive oil

### Instructions

1. In a bowl, crack the eggs open and beat for 3 minutes with a hand mixer.
2. In a non-stick pan, add 1 tsp of olive oil and pour in the whipped eggs. Cover and cook for about 2 minutes on low heat or until the eggs are cooked. It's going to be a fluffy omelet. Half-fold and slide over a plate.
3. Slice the mushrooms, dice the red pepper, and chop the Swiss chard. In a frying pan, heat the oil and add the red peppers. Cook, add the mushrooms and Swiss chard for a minute and cook until wilted. Sprinkle with salt, pepper, and powder of garlic. Place the folded omelet over it.

**Macros** - 263 calories 19.29g fat 8.56g carbs 2.4g fiber 5.26g sugar 14.98g protein

## LUNCH

## FLUFFY OMELETTE & VEGGIES

### Ingredients

- 1/2 zucchini (100g)

- 1/2 small cucumber
- 1/2 cup fresh spinach
- One hard-boiled egg
- 1 serving basil vinaigrette

### Instructions

1. Thinly slice the zucchini and cucumber with a cabbage shredder.
2. Cut the spinach into 4 and cut the egg.
3. Place all on a plate and pour over the dressing.

**Macros** - 296 calories 25.93g fat 9.16g carbs 2.3g fiber 3.53g sugar 9.05g protein

## DINNER

## ROASTED CHICKEN LEG & VEGGIES

### Ingredients

- Six asparagus spears (40g)
- 1/2 zucchini
- 100g mini carrots, Two chicken legs (600g)
- 1 tbsp olive oil, Six cherry tomatoes (80g)
- 1/4 tsp salt, black pepper, cumin, paprika, chili powder

### Instructions

1. Preheat to 200C/400F for the oven.
2. Cut off the asparagus from the roots. Slice the courgettes into vertical slices. Slice in half the mini carrots. In a 10 "cast iron skillet, put all the vegetables. Cover with the two legs of the hen. Pour over all the olive oil. Sprinkle the spices on both legs of the chicken.

3. Place the skillet in the oven and then bake uncovered for about 50 minutes.
4. Take it away and enjoy it. Keep half for a different meal.

**Macros** - 632 calories 37.78g fat 9.06g carbs 3g fiber 4.69g sugar 61.15g protein

# DAY 6

## BREAKFAST

## BACON, SPINACH & EGGS

### Ingredients

- Three slices of bacon (40g cooked)
- Two eggs
- 30g spinach pinch salt, pepper

### Instructions

1. Up to crispy, cook the bacon.
2. Cut the spinach and add the bacon to the frying pan. Cook until wilted in the bacon grease. Crack over the spinach the eggs open, cover, and cook for 2-3 minutes until the whites are fully cooked.
3. Sprinkle the eggs with salt and pepper. Slide down to a bacon plate.

**Macros** - 354 calories 25.52g fat 2.39g carbs 0.7g fiber 0.9g sugar 27.14g protein

## LUNCH

## CHICKEN MEATBALL LETTUCE CUPS

### Ingredients

- Four lettuce leaves two chicken meatballs 1/4 tomato 1/2 avocado

1/2 tbsp mayo 1/2 tbsp dijon pinch of parsley

### Instructions

1. Tomato dice and avocado dice. Cut the four pieces of meatballs. Place on top of each other two leaves of lettuce.
2. In a small bowl, mix the mayo and dijon. Spread half of it on every cup.
3. In each lettuce cup, add half of the meatballs, tomato, and avocado. Attach a little chopped parsley to it all.

**Macros** - 599 calories 44.65g fat 17.04g carbs 9.6g fiber 3.73g sugar 36.57g protein

## DINNER

## GRILLED SALMON, RADISHES & GREEN BEANS

### Ingredients

- 1 tsp of olive oil, 150g of salmon fillet, 50g green beans,
- 1 tsp olive oil, 1/4 tsp dill, salt, black pepper, 1 tsp lemon juice
- Five radishes (85g)
- 1 tbsp of rosemary pinch salt, pepper, garlic powder
- One garlic clove, 2 tsp olive oil pinch salt, pepper

### Instructions

1. Use the butter, dill, salt, and pepper to smooth the salmon.
2. Place carefully in a non-stick frying pan and cook for 2-3 minutes on both sides until thoroughly cooked. Add the lemon juice over the salmon once cooked.
3. Mince the clove of the garlic. Boil the green beans and cook for 5-6

minutes. Take the frying pan with the olive oil out of the water and add the chopped garlic. Sprinkle the salt and pepper and cook until the garlic is crispy in the frying pan. In a frying pan, heat the olive oil, add the radishes, and the rosemary. Cook until crispy 4-5 minutes. Sprinkle with salt and chili pepper.

4. 4. Serve it all on a plate together and enjoy it.

**Macros** - 415 calories 26.8g fat 9.04g carbs 3.7g fiber 2.73g sugar 34.3g protein

# DAY 7

## BREAKFAST

## SAUSAGE, EGG & CHEESE

## Ingredients

- 3 oz. breakfast sausage (e.g., Jimmy Dean)
- 1 large egg
- 1 tbsp olive oil
- 1 slice cheddar cheese
- Chives or green onion for garnish

## Instructions

1. Cook the sausage and egg in a lightly oiled pan (sunny side up or over easy).
2. Arrange with a slice of cheddar and drizzle, if you like, with some hot sauce.
3. Garnish with chives or green onion.

**Macros** - Calories: 574, 49F, 27P, 1C

## LUNCH

## EASY COBB SALAD

## Ingredients

- 1 large hard-boiled egg
- 4 oz. chicken breast
- 1 cup spinach, 2 strips bacon
- ¼ avocado
- 1 tbsp olive oil, ½ tsp white vinegar

## Instructions

1. Cook the egg for 10 minutes, bring a pot of water to boil. Cool it in cold water once it is cooked and chop it.
2. Heat 4 oz on a saucepan. From the chicken breast to the bacon.
3. Chop or rip the leaves of spinach and add to the bacon, chicken, and chopped egg.
4. Throw an avocado in half and mix to break it down.
5. Use a low carb Bleu cheese dressing or dress with olive oil and vinegar.

**Macros** - Calories: 600, 48F, 43P, 2C

## DINNER

## SRIRACHA LIME FLANK STEAK

## Ingredients

- 7 oz. asparagus, 8 oz. flank steak
- Salt, pepper
- Sriracha Lime Sauce
- ½ lime 1 tbsp sriracha, ½ tsp vinegar
- Salt, pepper, 1 tbsp olive oil

## Instructions

1. Trim the ends off the asparagus and allow them to fry for about 10 minutes on medium heat, often tossing.
2. Using salt & pepper for seasoning the steak liberally. Broil for medium-rare 5 minutes on each hand. For

medium and well-done, add 1 minute on each side and 2 minutes.

3. Cover the steak and allow 5 minutes to rest. Alternatively, blend with sriracha, vinegar, salt, & pepper and squeeze fresh lime in a pan. Slowly pour in olive oil while whisking these together to create an emulsion and thicken the sauce.

4. Slice thin steak and serve with asparagus and sauce. Enjoy

**Macros** - Calories: 560, 34F, 52P, 8C

CPSIA information can be obtained
at www.ICGtesting.com
Printed in the USA
LVHW060724141020
668669LV00017BA/1048